GREEK AND LATIN LYRIC POETRY IN TRANSLATION

GREEK AND LATIN LYRIC POETRY IN TRANSLATION

RICHARD TARRANT

AMERICAN PHILOLOGICAL ASSOCIATION
1972

Design/Pamela Patrick

Manufactured in The United States of America

The American Philological Association
Foreign Languages Building
University of Illinois
Urbana, Illinois

CONTENTS

Introduction	1
Anthologies of Greek Lyric Poetry	5
The Greek Anthology	11
Archilochus	15
Pindar	17
Sappho	20
Theocritus	24
Anthologies of Latin Lyric Poetry	25
Catullus	27
Horace	38
Martial	41
Ovid, Amores	46
Propertius	50
Tibullus	55
Virgil, Eclogues	58
Afterword	59
Notes	60
Index	63

INTRODUCTION

It might be argued that in no other area of classical literature are the difficulties of translation greater or the risks of failure more insidious than in lyric poetry. Yet in recent years classical scholars have almost abandoned this field of translation to non-specialists: of the translations surveyed in this report, fewer than a quarter are the work of professional classicists. Even if one does not subscribe as I do to the dictum of Wilamowitz, 'nur der Philologe kann übersetzen', one must ask whether poets and professors of English, whose knowledge of Latin and Greek is rarely exact and whose impressions of ancient literature are often vague and out-of-date, are really the ideal translators of Greek and Latin poetry. In an older and, in this respect, perhaps better time, when the only sort of translation classical students and scholars took seriously was into Latin and Greek, it was possible to view the efforts of those who swam against the stream with detached amusement[1]; but classicists today cannot afford to ignore the form in which nearly all prospective students of ancient poetry will first encounter it. It simply will not do to call Pindar and Horace 'untranslatable'; they are, and will continue to be, translated, and the only question is how well the job will be done. The following report suggests that the task may be badly botched, with all that such a failure would imply for the future of classical studies, unless competent specialists show a more sympathetic attitude toward and assume a more active role in these efforts than they have thus far done.

This report is concerned with translations of Greek and Latin lyric, elegiac, and pastoral poetry; epigrams in elegiac metre are included, but didactic elegy (e.g., Ovid's *Ars Amatoria*) is not. All American and most English editions currently in print and known to me are reviewed,[2] with the following exceptions: I have limited myself to translations with a claim to literary merit, and so have excluded all prose renderings; versions couched in an archaic idiom have not been reviewed in detail—to the modern ear lines like 'Thou, Tityrus, 'neath the leafy beeches lying, / drawest wild wood-notes from thine oaten straw' belong to the category of humour, not poetry; finally, 'imitations' of ancient poets, in the manner of Pound's Propertius, have not been treated.

The editions have been evaluated from only one standpoint, their suitability as texts for the study of ancient poetry. For this purpose I have regarded the best translation as the one which permits the largest number of correct conclusions to be drawn regarding the poetic qualities of its original—theme, tone, level of language, movement—and which introduces the fewest alien poetic elements. This is not the only standard which might be applied to translations of poetry, and in some instances in the following survey it is not the one by which the translator would wish to be judged, but it is the ideal that must be aimed at by all who teach ancient poetry in translation.

In treating each translation I have tried both to describe and to evaluate, and to express no judgements, particularly negative ones, without citing specific examples. For the convenience of non-specialist readers, however, most detailed comment involving citation of Latin or Greek text has been typographically segregated. At the end of most assessments I have referred, in a paragraph entitled 'other opinion', to at least one review of the translation just considered, to alert readers to divergent or supporting views; these references were collected only after my own appraisals were in their final form. To conserve space I occasionally do not give the original text of an example, assuming that my readers will have ready access to the relevant editions. In describing metrical forms I use a simple shorthand (iambic pentameter = ia^5, and so on), and in notating rhyme-schemes the symbol *x* designates unrhymed verse-endings (e.g., 'storm-part-rudder-heart' would be xaxa).

ANTHOLOGIES OF GREEK LYRIC POETRY

GREEK LYRIC POETRY, transl. Willis Barnstone, introduction and notes by William McCulloh. Bloomington (Ind.): Indiana University Press 1961 (repr. 1967). Pp. 310; $6.75 cloth. New York: Schocken Books 1972. $2.95 paper.
Free verse, 614 items. The introduction (pp. 1-13) gives a rather breathless survey of Greek Lyric in which analogies with modern European poetry play a larger than usual role; the translator contributes a note explaining his principle of selection ('lyric' is rather unhelpfully defined as 'a short poem that sings'). Each poet, however minor, is introduced by a biographical sketch, and for most one or more ancient *testimonia* are cited. There is a full glossary (pp. 263-291), a poorly-focused bibliography, and an elaborate set of concordances to Edmonds, Diehl, and, where relevant, *Poetae Melici Graeci* ('Page') and *Poetarum Lesbiorum Fragmenta* ('Lobel and Page').[3]

This is easily the most extensive anthology of Greek lyric now available, and because of its introductions and notes it is probably also the most useful for teaching purposes. Its superiority to Lattimore's *Greek Lyrics* consists mainly in its coverage of Greek lyric after the fifth century, in particular in its generous sampling from the *Anthology*; even in the early period, however, Barnstone gives considerably more material than Lattimore, especially from Archilochus, Alcman, Sappho, Alcaeus, Stesichorus, Ibycus, Hipponax, and Anacreon. But in spite of its bulk (nearly four times the size of Lattimore's book), the collection is not without its gaps; the more serious are mentioned here in the hope that the later edition spoken of on p. 16 may rectify them. Some of the most famous and important specimens of early elegy and iambic are missing—Solon's prayer to the Muses, Semonides on women, Xenophanes on athletics—, an omission not wholly justified by Barnstone's claim that 'the longer poems in elegiac couplets tend at times. . .to become essays in verse' (p. 16, n. 2). The decision to limit Pindar to three short *epinicia* (*Ol.* 3, 11, 12) is unfortunate; a better notion of his poetry could have been given by two or three of the greatest pieces. Bacchylides's *epinicia* are also slighted; with the complete translation by Fagles now unavailable, this should be corrected. Simonides's poem on Aretê for Scopas and the Attic *scolia* are also absent. More serious are deficiencies in the Hellenistic treatment: the definition of 'lyric' should not be so strict as to admit Callimachus only as an epigrammatist or to exclude the *Idylls* of Theocritus. Among the poets of the *Anthology* Plato, Meleager, and Lucilius are well-represented, while one could wish for more from Asclepiades, Leonidas, Rufinus, Palladas, Paulus Silentiarius, and Agathias. Space might be found for some of these additions by excising the poets whose remains are not substantial enough to give either pleasure or instruction, and who are included only because of their early date—Apollodorus, Asios, Hipparchus, Hippon, Lamprocles, Melanippides, Telesilla, and (if the *Persae* be excluded) Timotheus.

As a translator Barnstone is not wild or arbitrary, but he is more prone than Lattimore to small alterations.

A sample piece, *A.P.* 9.363 (Meleager), contained more than a score of such changes in a poem of twenty-three lines. Of these some may be thought slight or defensible (4 *νέοις* 'tiny'; 5 *ἀεξιφύτου* untranslated; 8 *ἐπιτέρπεται* 'gloats over'; 20 *τέρπεται* 'meander'); but several are significant changes of imagery or sense (1 *οἰχομένοιο* 'are drained out'; 3 *ἐστέψατο* 'glitters'; 4 *ἐκόμησε* 'pop open'; 9 *πλώουσιν* 'race across'; 19 *φυτῶν χαίρουσι κόμαι* 'saplings blossom'; 21 *ναῦται πλώουσι* 'fleets scud on the sea'; 22 *μέλπει* 'dazzle the sky with song'; 23 *πῶς οὐ χρὴ καὶ ἀοιδὸν ἐν εἴαρι καλὸν ἀεῖσαι;* 'why can a singer not praise the lovely spring?').

These changes show clearly enough that Barnstone is not prepared, as an English poet, to respect the comparatively generic descriptive language of Greek poetry. This policy is not in itself objectionable, but it is one of which users of this collection should remain aware. Barnstone is not the equal of Lattimore at his best, but the range of his selection goes far to offset this deficiency.

[Other opinion. D. Parker (*CW* 56 [1962] 43) is generally favourable, but notes occasional 'over-blandness' and misleading poem-titles.]

⁂ GREEK LYRICS, transl. Richmond Lattimore. 2nd rev. ed. Chicago: University of Chicago Press 1960. Pp. xvi, 82; $4.00 cloth; $1.50 paper.

Free verse. A compact preface (pp. iv-vi) lists the kinds of poetry denoted by the inexact modern term 'lyric', and gives the place of origin of their major practitioners. A map (pp. xii-xiii) is a welcome feature, but this one would be more useful if it did not fail to label such places as Thrace, Troy, Smyrna, Chios, Samos, Rhodes, Delos, Euboea, and Mycenae. There are concordances, and brief introductions to the individual poets. These do not avoid error or doubtful assertion (Archilochus 'made his living as a mercenary soldier'; 'the poems [of the Theognidean corpus] addressed to Kyrnos... are the ones most likely to belong to Theognis himself'), but convey much useful information efficiently. There are no notes or glossary.

Lattimore's selection is small, but almost no space in this book is wasted. The range is limited—Archilochus to the end of the fifth century—and the coverage is generally fair with the glaring exception of Pindar, who is represented only by fragments, mostly of paeans and dirges (a reluctance to impinge on the sales of the translator's separate edition of the *epinicia* may explain this gap). Lattimore is especially generous in his treatment of early elegy (pp. 7-31), which he translates excellently. His handling of lyric proper is less even; Sappho in particular suffers from inaccuracy, excessive restoration, and clumsy phrasing.

L.-P. 1.9 'sparrows, who *fairly* drew you...' (= κάλοι ?); 11f. 'the bright air/trembling *at the heart* (= διὰ μέσσω ?); 15f. the important repeated δηὖτε is missed; L.-P. 16.9 'fled away to Troy-land across the water'; 18 'the *shining pallor* of her face (ἀμάρυχμα λάμπρον); L.-P. 31.3f. 'its sweetness/murmur in love and/laughter, *all for him* (= πλάσιον ?); 11f. 'my ears *are/muted in thunder*' (ἐπιρρόμβεισι δ' ἄκουαι); 14f. 'paler I turn than grass is'; L.-P. 96.4f. 'she adored you (= ἀριγνώται) as *symbol of some* divinity (θέαι...ἰκέλαν), Arignota' (!); 7f. 'as/into dark when the sun has set/the moon, *pale-handed* (= βροδοδάκτυλος), at last appeareth/making dim all the rest of the stars'.

In the other lyric poets such lapses are less frequent; Bacchylides in particular is both well-represented and generally well translated. The book's strongest feature, though, is its elegiac section; here it is not displaced by Barnstone's larger anthology. [Other opinion: L.E. Woodbury (*CW* 50 [1957] 102) praises Lattimore's scholarship and taste: 'he amplifies only a little, and omits even less'.]

✻ GREEK POETRY, transl. F.L. Lucas, New York: Dutton Everyman Series 1966. Pp. xxxviii, 250; $2.95.
Rhymed lines (mostly abab, aabb etc.) of various lengths. The editorial apparatus is exceptionally full and helpful: the introduction includes an essay on Greece and Greek culture, a chronological table, a good discussion of Greek metre and the possibilities for its approximation in English, and an exposition of the aim and method of the selection; each of the book's four sections (Hesiod and Homeric Hymns, Archilochus to Alexander, Alexandrian Period, Roman and Early Byzantine Period) is followed by notes, and each author is sketched and briskly evaluated; there are appendixes on the *Palatine Anthology* and the Delphic oracle (pp. 239-249). Throughout Lucas's wide knowledge of English and European poetry is in evidence; many helpful parallels and comparisons are made.

Lucas is an articulate and engaging editor, but his book

cannot be commended to students. The selection seriously slights early lyric in favour of the often trivial epigrams of the *Anthology*, and in all the translations a somewhat old-fashioned, Golden Treasury diction and style are used.

Two examples from the *Anthology* will show the result. Plato's epigram on Lais (6.1) ends *ἐπεὶ τοίη μὲν ὁρᾶσθαι/οὐκ ἐθέλω, οἵη δ'ἦν πάρος οὐ δύναμαι*, which Lucas renders 'since now to see my likeness, as it is, grows past enduring;/since I no more may see it, as in old days it was'; *A.P.* 5.169.3f. (Asclepiades) *ἥδιον δ' ὁπόταν κρύψῃ μία τοὺς φιλέοντας/χλαῖνα, καὶ αἰνῆται Κύπρις ὑπ' ἀμφοτέρων* becomes 'yet sweeter beneath one mantle when lover lies by lover/and both, O Love, breathe blessings upon the name of Thee'.

❦ OXFORD BOOK OF GREEK VERSE IN TRANSLATION, ed. C.M. Bowra and T.F. Higham. Oxford: Oxford University Press 1938. Pp. cxii, 781; £2.10 (U.S. $9.50). Many translators and styles; 706 items. The introduction falls into three sections: Bowra on the character and development of Greek poetry (ix-xxxii), Higham on Greek poetry in translation, an important and interesting essay which should be read by scholars and by prospective translators (xxxiii-ciii), and a short section on proper names (cix-cxii). The notes (pp. 677-760) explain the context of selections, cite parallels, and record divergences from the text printed in the *Oxford Book of Greek Verse*. There are indexes of poets and translators, and a list giving the source of each translation.

Considering the range of the anthology (Homer to Cometas) and the inclusion of epic and drama, the coverage given to lyric is surprisingly full. Archilochus, Solon, and Stesichorus, however, are under-represented, Sappho L.-P. 2 and 16 are missing, and of the major poets of the *Anthology* only Meleager and Palladas receive adequate attention. A more serious complaint concerns the policy of giving *morceaux choisis* from the larger forms: no complete epinician ode of Pindar or hymn of Callimachus is included, and both Bacchylides and Theocritus are represented largely by excerpts.

The translations vary widely. Those by the editors are always at least acceptable, often better; Bowra's tend to be plain and serviceable, Higham's lively and free. But there are too many versions in a style impossible to take seriously in a modern publication, e.g., those by W. Leaf, F.E. Garrett, C.J. Billson, W.H.D. Rouse, and G. Highet. The notes are sound and useful.

⁂ SWANS AND AMBER. SOME EARLY GREEK LYRICS FREELY TRANSLATED AND ADAPTED, transl. Dorothy B. Thompson. Toronto: University of Toronto Press 1948. Pp. xii, 192; $3.25.
Rhymed stanzas of four to six verses. The range is from Archilochus to Bacchylides, the arrangement is by geographical regions. Longer poems are not represented (e.g., Alcman's *Partheneion*, Solon's prayer to the Muses, the *epinicia* of Pindar and Bacchylides). The translations are too loose and 'pretty' for our purposes; many are restorations, often with several fragments (possibly unrelated) joined and surrounded by new material (these additions are marked).

The following anthologies are unacceptable: they contain an inadequate selection of lyrics, and employ archaic or pseudo-archaic translations.

Portable Greek Reader, ed. W.H. Auden. New York: Viking 1949. Pp. viii, 726; $1.85 paper.
Greek Literature in Translation, ed. George Howe, G.A. Harrer, P.H. Epps. 2nd rev. ed. New York: Harper and Row 1948. Pp. xviii, 903; $10.95.
Greek and Roman Classics in Translation, ed. W.J. Oates, C.T. Murphy, K. Guinagh, New York: Longmans, Green 1947. Pp. lvi, 1051.
Ancient Greek Literature in Translation, ed. Lewis A. Richards. Chicago: Argonaut 1966. 2 vols. Pp. 242, 187.
Classics of Greek Literature, ed. H.E. Wedeck. Littlefield, N.J.: Prentice-Hall 1964. $2.25 paper.

THE GREEK ANTHOLOGY

POEMS FROM THE GREEK ANTHOLOGY, transl. Dudley Fitts. New York: New Directions 1938 (repr. 1956). Pp. xix, 141; $1.95 paper.
Free verse; 141 items, arranged in no particular order, with *A.P.* numbers given in an index. The introduction (pp. xiv-xix) defends the freedom and modernity of the versions. No notes or glossary.

POEMS FROM THE GREEK ANTHOLOGY, transl. Kenneth Rexroth. Ann Arbor: University of Michigan Press 1962. Pp. 111; $1.75 paper.
Free verse; 111 items, about fifteen of them Latin poems (Martial and the *Anthologia Latina*), arranged by author in alphabetical order; *A.P.* numbers not given. In a foreword Rexroth explains the origins of his selection and the technique of translation used. No notes or glossary ('the poems themselves need no explication').

SELECTIONS FROM THE GREEK ANTHOLOGY, transl. Andrew Sinclair. New York: Macmillan 1967. Pp. 150; $4.95.
Short lines (ia^4 and tr^4 predominate) with rhyme (aabb, abab, xaxa); 350 items, in two sections: epigrams whose authors are known, arranged chronologically, and anonymous epigrams arranged by subject; *A.P.* numbers not given. The preface (pp. 13-17) states the appeal of the *Anthology* as 'an unequalled record of a civilisation'; a translator's note (pp. 18-20) discusses Sinclair's methods. No notes or glossary.

⁂ TWO HUNDRED POEMS FROM THE GREEK ANTHOLOGY, transl. Robin Skelton. London: Methuen, Toronto: McClelland and Stewart, Seattle: University of Washington Press 1971. Pp. xxi, 78; £1.25 (Canada $4.50).
Ia^4, ia^5, tr^4, and tr^5 with various rhyme-schemes; the 200 items are arranged by author in alphabetical order, with *A.P.* numbers given after each poem. The introduction (p. vii-xxi) enumerates the books of the *A.P.* with their contents, and discusses the approach taken in the translation; much is made of the affinities between the *Anthology* and seventeenth-century English poetry, but no examples are discussed. No notes or glossary; index of poets.
A translation of the *Anthology* which faithfully mirrors its diversity of content and its conventionality of style is still to appear, and for obvious reasons. The translator who must select less than a tenth of the collection inevitably imposes his own bias in his choices; he will be attracted above all by one mood of these epigrams—erotic, satiric, sepulchral, or whatever—, and he will have neither the space nor the interest to show how themes, once used, are refashioned by both small and large talents. The 'modernity' of the *Anthology*, attractive to translators and readers, is a temptation to free translation: surely, the argument seems to run, one may help an author who seems to think in such a familiar way to speak as a modern poet would?

These processes are at work in all the translations described above, nor are their authors unaware of them. Sinclair says he has chosen from the 'epigrams of bite and wit'; he has more selections from Palladas than from Callimachus and Meleager combined. His style is adapted to this slanted outlook: terse and clipped, with much more than connectives and particles shorn away. It is, however, a somewhat brittle instrument, able to handle well the shorter sallies of Lucilius or Nicarchus, and producing at times an improving compression (e.g., in Meleager's πταίης μοι, κώνωψ [5.152], p. 44), but frigid when dealing with pathos or complex feeling: Callimachus's famous epigram on Heraclitus (7.80; p. 30) swerves at the end from stiff-upper-lip dryness to schoolgirl lyricism:

> When they told me you were gone,
> I remembered how the sun,
> Heraclitus, time and again
> set on our talks:[4] and I wept then.
> Halicarnassus saw you born.
> Somewhere, dust now picks your bone.
> But, though Death takes everything,
> Your *Nightingales* still sing, ah sing.

A different failing reveals itself in Sinclair's version of *Ἂν μνήμην, ἄνθρωπε, λάβῃς, ὁ πατήρ σε τί ποιῶν/ἔσπειρεν, παύσῃ τῆς μεγαληφροσύνης* (10.45.1f., p. 86): 'Remember, man, your father's cock. Does vanity survive the shock?' Here rhyme, which Sinclair does not handle without awkwardness, has led him to falsify a significant aspect of his original: like Juvenal, Palladas here expresses scatological thoughts while avoiding *verba praefanda*. These two examples also demonstrate the degree of freedom to add and omit which Sinclair allows himself even in the narrow confines of his chosen form.

Skelton is equally forthright about his preferences: he exalts the erotic, convivial, and satiric, and slights the sepulchral, declamatory, and dedicatory (p. xvii); he also allows himself to modernise names, diction, and allusions where the tone is 'informal' (i.e., in the great majority of his selections). His is in fact the freest of the four editions under review, with only occasional lapses into straight translation (e.g., 10.4, p. 34). He is best with short, witty epigrams, where his greater flexibility often gives him an edge over Sinclair (e.g., 5.45, p. 13; 11.139, p. 29; 11.138 and 94, p. 31; 10.98, p. 43; 11.418, p. 71). In longer love-poems his tendency to pad or alter the imagery becomes alarming (e.g., Asclepiades 5.169, p. 8: *ἡδύ...ἡδύ...ἥδιον* wonderful. . .marvellous. . .triumphant'; *καὶ αἰνῆται* Κύπρις ὑπ' ἀμφοτέρων 'warm/on an April hill'; also Asclepiades 5.85, 189, p. 7f.; Meleager 5.152, 156, 166, 171, 173, pp. 35-38; Paulus Silentiarius 5.232, 253, 275, 283, pp. 46-50; Rufinus 5.21, 27, 36, 41, pp. 58-61; Strato 12.15, 205, 211, 227, pp. 65-70). It should be remarked, though, that some of Skelton's unfaithful renderings are better English poems than a close translation could have produced (e.g., Rufinus 5.37, 42, 44, pp. 59-62).

The selections of Fitts and Rexroth are shorter than the foregoing, but more representative: amatory, satiric, sepulchral, and dedicatory epigrams are all fairly evenly present. These editions are also alike in their inconsistency; they contain both perfectly straight translation and loose paraphrase, with no means for the non-specialist to tell them apart. Rexroth is best at the erotic poems, some of which he does better than any other translator; Fitts excels at the epigrams of wit and satire, where his cleverness and typographical mannerisms become positive features.

In general none of the separate editions of the *Anthology* now available offers a selection markedly superior to that of Barnstone, whose notes on the individual epigrammatists are an additional advantage. It is unfortunate that no translator of the *Anthology*, Barnstone included, alludes to its importance for the understanding of Latin lyric, elegy, and epigram from Catullus to Martial.

[Other opinion. *Rexroth*: D. Parker, *CW* 56 (1962) 43, 'one reads it for Rexroth (who is eminently worth it).' *Sinclair*: Averil Cameron, *CW* 62 (1968) 27, 'This is not the *Anthology*, but all the same, it is a modern, unsentimental and interesting collection.']

ARCHILOCHUS

CARMINA ARCHILOCHI: THE FRAGMENTS OF ARCHILOCHUS, transl. Guy Davenport. Berkeley: University of California Press 1964. Pp. xxi, 104; $1.50 paper. $4.00 cloth.

Free verse. A foreword by Hugh Kenner (pp. vii-xi) rejoices that the current unromantic approach to the Greeks makes a just assessment of Archilochus possible. The introduction (pp. xiii-xix) deals with Archilochus's life and later reputation. The Budé edition of Lasserre and Bonnard is used as a base, with some scraps left out and some poems added from Edmonds and Diehl. The Budé numbering, however, is not used (why?), and a concordance is given (pp. 98-104).

To translate all the fragments of Archilochus would daunt anyone aware of the uncertainties of text and interpretation involved. Davenport claims only 'an amateur's Greek' and possesses no specialised knowledge of ancient literature;[5] he is sustained by his own poetic talents and his willingness to improvise where the transmitted text fails him. The results are lively and readable English poems, but only where the text is secure, and not always then, are they translations in our sense. The concordance does frequently state or hint that the English incorporates conjectural reconstruction or original ideas, but by no means all such cases are noted: e.g., 16 (L.-B. 114), 36 (L.-B. 184), 113 (L.-B. 82), 121 (L.-B. 1, almost unrecognisable), 129 (given as = L.-B. 4; actually it combines 3 and 4 with much added material), 146 (L.-B. 46), 195 (L.-B. 42; a completely independent poem), 231 (L.-B. 117), 286 (L.-B. 239). A non-specialist can never be sure what in this book is Archilochus and what is Davenport (or Bonnard), and for teaching purposes this is a fatal objection.

On the other hand, many of Archilochus's most famous pieces are handled as well or better by Davenport than by the anthologies which are his only rival: among the successes are 2 (L.-B. 7), 14 (L.-B. 15), 23 (L.-B. 123), 29 (L.-B. 266), 57 (L.-B. 5), 72 (L.-B. 118), 110 (L.-B. 10), 168 (L.-B. 120), 174 (L.-B. 282), 184 (L.-B. 14), 205 (L.-B. 11), 213 (L.-B. 122), 260 (L.-B. 159), 282 (L.-B. 93). The book should therefore be consulted by specialists, who will be able to distinguish the worthwhile from the speculative or meretricious.

[Other opinion. Davenport was charged with fanciful and inaccurate translation by A. Pippin Burnett (*CP* 60 [1965] 49f.) and A.D. Fitton Brown (*JHS* 85 [1965] 173f).]

PINDAR

THE ODES OF PINDAR, transl. C.M. Bowra. Harmondsworth (Middlesex): Penguin Books 1969. Pp. 256; £0.35 paper (U.S. $1.45).
All the epinician odes are included, in Bowra's opinion of their chronological order; free verse. The introduction (pp. ix-xviii) deals with Pindar's life and historical surroundings, his relations with his patrons, and the form, style, and themes of his poetry. A useful list of events at the great games is appended. Each poem is followed by a very brief section of notes. A glossary helpfully distinguishes mythical from historical figures.

THE ODES OF PINDAR, transl. Richmond Lattimore. Chicago: University of Chicago Press 1947. Pp. xii, 170; $1.95 paper, $4.25 cloth.
All the epinician odes are included, in the MSS arrangement; free verse. The introduction (pp. v-xii) discusses the conditions under which Pindar composed and examines some typical structural devices. A section of notes (pp. 151-160) gives each ode's date and addressee, with the briefest of characterisations. A glossary is given (pp. 161-170).

PINDAR: SELECTED ODES, transl. with interpretive essays by Carl A.P. Ruck and William H. Matheson. Ann Arbor: University of Michigan Press 1968. Pp. 269; $10.00.
Twenty-one odes are included (*Ol.* 1, 2, 4, 6, 7, 10, 11, 14; *Pyth.* 1-4, 8, 9, 12; *Nem.* 3, 6, 7; *Isth.* 5, 6, 8) in an order which is said to 'move from simpler to more complex

structures' (p. 13), though beginning with *Pyth.* 4 and ending with *Isth.* 5 and 6. Free verse. Each ode is preceded by an essay which explores certain of its features; the essays vary in length from twenty pages (*Pyth.* 4) to three pages (*Isth.* 8), with ten pages the average length. The treatment is purely literary, and no attempt is made to discuss points of difficulty or textual uncertainty.[6] There is no general essay on Pindar's life or poetry, and no notes or glossary. The introduction deals entirely with the problem of translating Pindar, though the points raised might be applied as well to any ancient author. The translators gleefully demolish some straw men ('literal translation', 'modern free translation') before setting forth their own unsurprising views: translation must proceed from thorough understanding, and can succeed only with a reader who is prepared to react properly. Hence the essays, which serve as 'indoctrination' and which, it is claimed, 'are not ancillary but are part of the total composition' (p. 13).

The versions of Bowra and Lattimore are both of high quality, but I confess to a preference for the greater concentration and richness of Lattimore's English.

Some examples: *Ol.* 7.7f. *ἐν δὲ φίλων/παρέοντων θῆκέ νιν ζαλωτὸν ὁμόφρονος εὐνᾶς* 'render him among friends present admired for the bride's consent' (Lattimore), 'makes him to be admired before his dear ones for his wedding in which two hearts are one' (Bowra); 9 *γλυκὺν καρπὸν φρενός* 'the mind's sweet yield' (Lattimore), 'sweet fruit of the heart' (Bowra)'; 94f. *ἐν δὲ μιᾷ μοίρᾳ χρόνου/ἄλλοτ' ἀλλοῖαι διαιθύσσοισιν αὖραι* 'but in one parcel of time/the winds inter-shifting flare to new directions' (Lattimore), 'in a single moment of time/many are the winds that blow this way and that' (Bowra); *Pyth.* 1.8 *ἀγκύλῳ κρατί* 'on his hooked head' (Lattimore), 'on his head and beak' (Bowra).

Against this, though, must be set Bowra's closer adherence in many passages to the actual meaning.

For example: *Ol.* 7.31 *αἱ δὲ φρενῶν ταραχαί* 'the heart's confusions' (Bowra), 'despair in the brain' (Lattimore); *Pyth.* 1.9 *τεαῖς/ῥιπαῖσι κατασχόμενος* 'your quivering song has conquered him' (Bowra), 'bound in spell of your waves' (Lattimore); *Pyth.* 8.15 *βία δὲ καὶ μεγάλαυχον ἔσφαλεν ἐν χρόνῳ* 'but Force trips up/at last even the loud boaster' (Bowra), 'but violence and high vaunting fail at the last' (Lattimore); 59 *ὑπάντασεν ἰόντι γᾶς ὀμφαλὸν παρ' ἀοίδιμον* 'He met me in my road/to earth's renownèd Navel' (Bowra), 'he met me in the way as I went to the singing centrestone of the earth' (Lattimore).

On balance I find Lattimore's inaccuracies neither numerous nor serious enough to offset his more skilful writing, but this judgement may not be shared by all readers.

Because of their unevenness the translations by Ruck and Matheson cannot contend with those just considered. Many lines are rendered with skill and imagination (e.g., *Pyth.* 8.15 'Braggadocio's violence trips him up, if given time'), but the reader is too often confused by obscurities that owe nothing to Pindar and affronted by ungainly expressions.

To avoid unfairness I give examples drawn from *Pyth.* 8 alone, a typical performance: 11f. *τιθεῖς/ὕβριν ἐν ἄντλῳ* 'to bilge/the troublemaker's insolence'; 21f. *ἔπεσε δ' οὐ Χαρίτων ἑκὰς/ἁ δικαιόπολις. . .νᾶσος* 'a lucky throw not far/from Grace this island, this Justice citadel'; 32 *μὴ κόρος ἐλθὼν κνίξῃ* 'boredom grates'; 34f. *ἴτω. . .ἐμᾷ ποτανὸν ἀμφὶ μαχανᾷ* 'O soar. . .on wing of art'; 76 *δαίμων δὲ παρίσχει* 'god is their provenience'; 96f. *ἀλλ' ὅταν αἴγλα διόσδοτος ἔλθῃ/λαμπρὸν φέγγος ἔπεστιν ἀνδρῶν καὶ μείλιχος αἰών* 'But when the sunburst Zeus gift comes, a/lambent aureole/rests on men and life is balm'.

The essays do not come within the scope of this review. Scholars will find in them useful and provocative ideas, but also much of less value: idle thoughts not worth pressing, forced schemata, banalities wrapped in jargon. They should not be given to students with no previous familiarity with Pindar.

[Other opinion. *Lattimore*: condemned by G. Norwood (*CP* 43 [1948] 60f.) for being in free verse and for inaccuracy in details; a more favourable verdict was rendered by J.A. Davison (*JHS* 67 [1947] 138: 'L. has made a gallant and remarkably successful attempt to solve the insoluble. . .can be read with pleasure and instruction.' *Ruck-Matheson*: both M.M. Willcock (*CR* N.S. 21 [1971] 13f.) and D.E. Gerber (*CW* 62 [1968] 105f.) find the essays worth the attention of Pindarists, the translations eccentric and inconsistent.]

SAPPHO

SAPPHO. A NEW TRANSLATION, transl. Mary Barnard. Berkeley: University of California Press 1958. Pp. x, 114; $1.25 paper.
Free verse; 100 items. Commendatory foreword by Dudley Fitts. The translator furnishes a 'footnote' (pp. 95-106) discussing Sappho's relationship with her girls (the analogy of a *kapelmeister* [*sic*] or a Renaissance artist and his studio is suggested) and the problems of Sappho-*Überlieferung*. The notes give the source of each fragment and its number in Edmonds's edition, usually nothing more.

SAPPHO. POEMS AND FRAGMENTS, transl. Guy Davenport. Ann Arbor: University of Michigan Press 1965. Pp. xx, 79; $1.75 paper; $3.95 cloth.
Free verse; 210 items. The introduction (pp. vii-xx) attempts a sketch of seventh-century Ionian culture and sounds a protest against the reconstructions of Edmonds ('the Arthur Evans of literature'). The text used is *PLF*, though as in his Archilochus Davenport produces his own numeration. The 'notes' (pp. 71-79) are little more than a concordance to *PLF*.

THE POEMS OF SAPPHO, transl. Suzy Q. Groden. Indianapolis: Bobbs-Merrill (Library of Liberal Arts no. 214) 1966. Pp. xxviii, 153; $1.75 paper.
Free verse; 133 items. The introduction (pp. xi-xxii) deals sanely with Sappho's life and later reputation, discusses the metre and some technical features of her poetry, and even admits its weaknesses (egotism and monotony). A concordance gives equivalents for *PLF* and Edmonds. There is an

indifferent bibliography, a short section of notes commenting on doubtful attributions and textual uncertainties, and a glossary of proper names (few of which are found in Sappho's text).

⁂ THE LOVE SONGS OF SAPPHO, transl. Paul Roche. New York: Mentor (New American Library) 1966, Pp. 224; $0.95 paper.
Free verse, with approximations of sapphic stanzas in the longer poems; 169 items. The apparatus is elaborate: a long introduction (pp ix-xxv), an appendix on the difficulty of translating Sappho (pp. 143-148), a polemical discussion of the relation between metrical-accent and speech-accent in Greek and English (pp. 149-152), a tabulation of Sappho's metres with English stress equivalents (pp. 153-156), an annotated bibliography of earlier translations and critical studies (pp. 157-163), and notes on each poem or fragment, giving metre, source, and number in Edmonds, and discussing textual and other difficulties in some detail (pp. 164-223). All this material is presented with more enthusiasm than judgement; Greekless readers will be lost much of the time, and scholars, though they will discover the odd bit of new information, will find Roche an unreliable and excessively voluble guide to Lesbian poetry.

The study of Sappho in translation must be primarily concerned with a half-dozen long and important fragments (L.-P. 1, 2, 16, 31, 94, 96). These are already available in Barnstone's and Lattimore's[7] anthologies, and Barnstone includes as well all smaller fragments of any interest or significance.[8] None of the editions under review contains more comprehensive and reliable secondary information than the diligent student will collect for himself in Page and Bowra; to prove useful for our purposes, then, their versions of the major fragments must be superior to those of the anthologists. Only Groden can be judged acceptable by this criterion. Her language is accurate and authentically plain, and she is the most careful of all Sappho's translators in her treatment of the text: gaps are faithfully represented (producing a tantalising effect in L.-P. 94.22 f.), and generally the translation indicates the extent of a poem not all of whose stanzas survive in intelligible form. Her helpful introduction and sound notes constitute an added advantage. One only wishes she had reduced her selection by omitting the twenty-odd scraps with which it trails off and devoted the space to more of the sensible criticism displayed in the introduction; fragments like 'of the Muses' or 'Medea' reveal nothing about Sappho or her poetry. Mary Barnard's translations have an attractive simplicity, and in certain poems (L.-P. 1, 16) she surpasses Lattimore and Barnstone, but she inserts too many doubtful supplements and original ideas to be preferred to Groden. Finally, both Davenport and Roche fall below the standard for comparison set by Lattimore and Barnstone. Davenport can be a model of sobriety in dealing with the lacunae of L.-P. 16.11f., but elsewhere he injects new and at times bizarre images and expressions: the opening of L.-P. 1 sounds more like Lycophron than Sappho, 'God's wildering daughter, deathless Aphródita [*sic*], /a whittled perplexity your bright abstruse chair'; equally startling is the beginning of L.-P. 94, 'I longed for death. Misery the size of terror/was in her tears when we unclasped forever.'[9] Roche does not distinguish Edmonds from Sappho in his versions, and in addition his phrases often lack the accents of human speech, e.g., L.-P. 94.4f. 'What a terrible blow, what sadness!/ Sappho, I swear I leave you/absolutely against my will'; 7 'Go, be happy, good-bye'; L.-P. 16.17f. 'the way she walks, her lovable style,/the vivid movement of her face'.

[Other opinion. *Barnard*: R.A. Swanson (*CJ* 54 [1958/9] 281-282) praises 'a clear simplicity and a very appropriate quiet intensity'. *Davenport*: C. Fuqua (*CW* 59 [1966] 219), 'distinctly different. . .very suggestive'; reservations expressed on details (e.g., LP 1.1). *Groden*: Fuqua (*CW* 60 [1967] 389) commends her intelligence, honesty, freshness, and candour. *Roche*: Fuqua (*ibid.*) calls the edition 'spirited but not successful'.]

THEOCRITUS

THE IDYLLS OF THEOCRITUS, transl. Barriss Mills. Lafayette (Ind.): Purdue University Press 1963. Pp. xiii, 113; $2.95 cloth.

Free verse. The short introduction emphasises Theocritus's skill in character-drawing and his reversal of epic values. No notes or glossary.

Mills's is the only verse rendering of Theocritus currently available. It is perhaps best seen as a turning into modern free verse of the prose translation from Gow's great edition of 1950. Mills has quite sensibly taken Gow as a reliable guide to the meaning of the Greek, and, while avoiding Gow's artificial archaism[10], he reproduces him very closely indeed, sometimes word for word.[11] There is nothing to criticise in this: the language is clear and plain, the lines move well enough, and with Gow's help a high standard of accuracy is generally maintained. Indeed, reservations are excited mainly by Mills's defections from his source.

He rather frequently fails to translate words which Gow had properly rendered (e.g., 1.15 *οὐ θέμις*, 18 *ἀεί*, 20 *ἐπὶ τὸ πλέον ἵκεο*, 38 *μοχθίζοντι*, 56 *αἰπολικόν*, 59f. *κεῖται ἄχραντον*), and there are some inexplicable mistranslations (e.g., 1.36f. *ἀλλ' ὅκα μὲν τῆνον ποτιδέρκεται ἄνδρα γέλαισα/ἄλλοκα δ' αὖ ποτὶ τὸν ῥιπτεῖ νόον* 'she glances at one of them and smiles, but her thoughts/are on the other'; 85 *ἆ δυσερώς τις ἄγαν καὶ ἀμήχανος ἐσσί*, 'you're a foolish lover and a feeble one'; 3.43 *ἀπ' Ὄθρυος...ἐς Πύλον*, 'from Pylos/...to Othrys'; 4.9 *ἔφαθ' ἁ μάτηρ*, 'mother says'; 62f. *τό τοι γένος ἢ Σατυρίσκοις...ἢ Πάνεσσι...ἐρίσδει*; 'you come of the Satyr-kind/and can hold your own with the...Pans').

The translations, however, remain serviceable in spite of these defects.

[Other opinion. G. Roberts (*CJ* 59 [1964] 279) called this 'a fine job of reflecting Theocritus in Modern English', but objected to its description as verse.]

ANTHOLOGIES OF LATIN LYRIC POETRY

LATIN POETRY IN VERSE TRANSLATION, Ed. L.R. Lind. Boston: Houghton Mifflin 1957; Oxford: Oxford University Press 1967. Pp. xxxix, 438; $1.75 paper; £0.80. This is the only anthology of Latin poetry now available which deserves serious consideration; it cannot be recommended without reservation in its present form, and the following comments are given with a view towards suggesting changes. The range covered has the look of a *tour de force*—Ennius and Plautus to a seventeenth-century sacred sonnet. The book is in fact too inclusive: the mediaeval section is necessarily spotty, and the Renaissance items are mere curiosities. A better book might result from stopping at Ausonius, with the space thus saved (pp. 319-399) used to fill in the classical picture. Catullus and Horace's *Odes* could be better served: many interesting or important poems have been left out (e.g., Catullus 3, 7, 13, 36, 49, 50, etc.; Horace 1.10, 34, 37; 2.6, 16, 19; 3.5, 6, 9, 10, 16, 21, 25, 29, 30; 4.3, 5, 12), while on the other hand space is given to relatively slight works (e.g., Catullus 1, 14, 23, 55, 58b, 69, 107; Horace 1.18, 33, 38; 2.4, 5, 8).

The translations are mostly, but not entirely, modern, and are more variable in quality than even the nature of an anthology requires; there are some non-starters (e.g., Catullus 4, 10, 23, 31, 42, 51, 70, 72, 85, 96; Horace 1.3, 4, 5 [Bennett], 11, 24, 25 [Nims], 38; 3.1, 18). The practice of printing several versions of a single poem is commendable, but all the versions should have something both unique and worthwhile to offer. The *Eclogues* are generously represented (1, 2, 3, 4, 5, 9), but in six different styles. Propertius receives a suitably large section (pp. 177-217), and unity is achieved by relying almost exclusively on translations by Frances Fletcher. These are more accurate than Carrier's, but less tightly structured than Watt's (qq.vv.). The inclusion of all of Propertius IV at the expense of the three earlier books is a debatable choice. Tibullus is given adequate coverage, but one might cavil at the space allotted to book IV of the *Corpus Tibullianum* in Creekmore's arrangement. Ovid's *Amores* are slighted, and Marlowe's translations are used. The short selection from Martial is enlivened by the renderings attributed to 'T.W.M.' (= T.W. Melluish).

With revision to place the central figures in a clearer light and to make use of the translations produced since 1957, this could become a useful and enjoyable anthology.

[Other opinion. M.L. Clarke (*CR* N.S. 18 [1968] 319-321): 'both as an anthology of translations and as a guide to Latin literature of all periods it should have a wide appeal'.]

The following anthologies are unacceptable: they contain an inadequate selection of lyrics, and employ archaic or pseudo-archaic translations.

Portable Roman Reader, ed. B. Davenport. New York: Viking 1951. Pp. xi, 656; $2.25 paper.

Roman Readings, ed. M. Grant. Harmondsworth (Middlesex): Penguin Books 1958. Pp. 464; $1.45 paper.

Roman Literature in Translation, ed. K. Guinagh, A.P. Dorjahn. 2nd rev. ed. New York: McKay 1952. Pp. xviii, 822; $7.95 cloth.

Classics of Roman Literature, ed. H.E. Wedeck. Paterson (N.J.): Littlefield, Adams 1964. Pp. x, 556; $2.95 paper.

CATULLUS

THE POEMS OF CATULLUS, transl. James Michie. London: Rupert Hart-Davies 1969. Pp. 239; £2.10 cloth. Bilingual edition; various metrical structures, almost all with rhyme. The elegant introduction, by Robert Rowland, gives particular weight to the Alexandrianism of the *novi poetae*; stimulating in approach, it should be treated with reserve in details. There are brief notes and a glossary (pp. 222-239).

Michie's is the best available translation of Catullus. He handles his predominantly iambic metres with great skill, and so manages to stay quite close to the text while at the same time enjoying the advantages of clear formal structure. His English, especially in the lighter poems (e.g., 10), has just the right blend of informality and sophistication, and at its best does not read like a translation at all. The standard is high; the lapses (e.g., 31, 84) are not disasters. An occasional Anglicism may jar an American reader (e.g., 'sod' for *irrumator* in 10.12, 'orator at the bar' for *patronus* in 49.7). A more serious drawback in the framework of this survey is the price; a paperback edition of this book is highly desirable, for it deserves the widest circulation.

[Other opinion. M.L. Clarke (*CR* N.S. 21 [1971] 290-291) approves of Michie's agility and accuracy, but criticises the translation of 31; Steele Commager (*New York Times Book Review* August 15, 1971, 35), 'I think Michie's translation easily the best recent one'.]

ODI ET AMO. THE COMPLETE POETRY OF CATULLUS, transl. Roy Arthur Swanson. Indianapolis: Bobbs-Merrill (Library of Liberal Arts no. 114) 1959. Pp. xix, 133; $1.75 paper.

A loose ia[4] is the most common metre; elegiacs are often rendered by alternating ia[5] and ia[4]. The apparatus is elaborate: the introduction is aimed at the reader coming to Catullus for the first time and covers a wide range of topics with good sense, if not with unfailing accuracy; a bibliography follows, in which Syme's *Roman Revolution* and Thornton Wilder's *Ides of March* rub shoulders under the rubric 'political and historical perspective'; notes explain obscurities and point out cross-references; there is an extensive, though not exhaustive glossary, and a list of Latin first lines.

When Swanson's versions succeed, they combine accuracy with effective control of a clearly defined metrical form. The number of total successes is not large (11, 49, 68.1-40, 70, 76), but there is a considerably larger group of quite acceptable, though flawed, translations. His renderings suffer from two defects. The confining ia[4] often results in a pallid, thinned-out approximation of the original.

63.73 *iam iam dolet quod egi, iam iam paenitet* 'already I'm sorry for what I have done'; 65.23f. *atque illud prono praeceps agitur decursu,/huic manat tristi conscius ore rubor* 'the apple rûns its race,/ and blushes bloom upon her face'.

The second is an unwillingness to follow Catullus in the frank expression of strong emotion, with the substitution of cuteness or a cooler paraphrase.

E.g., 3.1f. 'Be blue, every Venus and Cupid,/and every sophisticate man'; 85 'I hate while I love; would you ask how I do it?/My pain proves it's true; that's all there is to it'; 101.5f. *quandoquidem fortuna mihi tete abstulit ipsum/heu miser indigne frater adempte mihi* 'since fate, where I'm concerned, has been so rash/as uselessly to hasten you away'.

Despite these shortcomings, instructors may wish to use this edition for its body of solid translations and its assortment of secondary material; both will need correction, but the proportion of truth to error is high enough to make the effort feasible.

[Other opinion. H.H. Bacon (*CW* 53 [1960] 231) judged Swanson's translation closer to the letter, but farther from the spirit of Catullus than that of Gregory.]

⁂ THE CARMINA OF CATULLUS, transl. Barriss Mills. Lafayette (Ind.): Purdue University Press 1965. Pp. 167; $4.95 cloth.

Free verse; lines are short, rarely containing more than four stresses. The introduction (pp. 9-20) is a thoughtful character-sketch of Catullus as an idealist and a romantic, with a tempering strain of irony. There is a welcome freedom from biographical interpretation,[12] and valid observations are made concerning Catullus's use of self-mockery, but the essay will yeild more profit to the student already familiar with the poems than to the beginner. No notes or glossary. The Latin texts of several poems[13] are included, apparently only to lend variety to the layout.

Mills's aim is best stated in his own words: 'my own strategy has been, first, to translate as literally as possible... and then to shape the results into idiomatic English having some rhythmic value' (p. 6). He has on the whole carried this plan to a successful conclusion, though the first part has been more consistently executed than the second. It is a relief to read translations content to let Catullus speak in his own words and images, and gratifying to see how much of his wit and elegance emerges from these studiously unadorned versions. But the method has the defects of its virtues. Mills's language will pass as verse in that it would read oddly if printed as prose, but one rarely finds the intense pressure on words that one associates with poetry. The use of free verse has a levelling effect: 63 is slowed down, 65 and 68 are unravelled, the contrast between the sapphics of 11 and 51 and the surrounding metres is missed. An occasional prosaic phrase jars: 8.8f. 'now she's not interested/anymore, and since there's nothing/you can do about it, you should be/ indifferent too, and not go chasing/after one who avoids you, making/your life a misery'; 76.13 'it's hard to give up suddenly/a friendship of long standing'. Finally Mills's commitment to the literal meaning at times leads him to translate the words at the expense of their intended effect: in 26 the pun on *opposita* has been lost, although the ambiguity in English 'draft' allows successful recreation of the joke in a freer version; the impact of 84 is considerably reduced by retaining *chommoda-commoda* and *insidias-hinsidias* rather than devising English equivalents.

In sum, while Mills offers more than a *dimidiatus Catullus*, he has aimed for and so achieved less than translation at its best can accomplish.

[Other opinion. H.J. Leon (*CW* 59 [1966] 201) found it reasonably close to the literal meaning (though inaccuracies were noted), but objected that it 'sounds more like prose than poetry'; R.A. Swanson, (*CJ* 62 [1966] 81f.) criticised errors of detail in the introduction and translations and summed up: 'about this version there is simply nothing distinctive or wholly fresh'.]

❧ CATULLUS: THE COMPLETE POETRY, transl. Frank O. Copley. Ann Arbor: University of Michigan Press 1957. Pp. xv, 141; $1.95 paper.

Free verse predominates in 1-60, 69-116; 61, 64-68 in ia^5, 62 in ia^4. The introduction (pp. v-xv) packs much matter into a short space. It is admirably skeptical on Catullan biography, including the identity of Lesbia; on Catullus's *doctrina* there is perhaps insufficient caution ('it is doubtful that he had read much more than any other cultivated man of his times...he is as much an "imitator" of Sappho and Archilochus and Homer as he is of the Alexandrians' p. x); there is also a well-written discussion of Catullus's place in what was shortly afterwards called the 'Catullan revolution' (pp. xii-xiv). The notes (pp. 123-141) contain helpful remarks on *Realien*, literary genres, and the structure of the long poems.

Copley's translation has suffered from the notoriety of a portion of its renderings, those in which Catullus is done into the outward dress of e e cummings. Two of these (7, 13) have recently been singled out as specimens of 'how not to translate Catullus' for the instruction of schoolboys;[14] this judgement is harsh, but fair, for these translations are wrong-headed and worthless. They do not recreate the spirit of the originals, nor are they interesting English poems, since Copley's use of cummingseque devices remains wholly external, never quickened by cummings's feeling for words. A second group, related to these and equally unsuccessful, employs a self-consciously vulgar tone and a sort of Newyorkese dialect (e.g. 53.5 *di magni, salaputium disertum* 'boyoboy can dat lidl squoit/make wid duh lengwich').[15] Copley's edition has become so widely identified with these renderings that it is surprising to discover how many poems do not fit the stereotype. Four further styles can be distinguished. The deliberately overblown is used in 11 and 63; in both cases there is justification in the poems, but Catullus's departures from this tone are not rendered. Archaic and stilted language appears in 34 and 63; again, one sees the rationale while feeling that the procedure does not quite work. Artificial literalism is employed for poetic effect in 51 and 76 (e.g., 51.10f. *sonitu suopte/tintinant aures* 'with their own sound/ roar my ears'; 76.13 *difficile est longum subito deponere amorem* 'it's hard long suddenly love to lay aside'), but the result only sounds like a speech impediment. Finally there is a large group of 'straight' translations (some tarted up by eccentric typography, but straight nonetheless), among which are several successes (8, 39, 43, 48, 50, 84) and a larger number which fall just below that level (36, 42, 70, 83, 85, 86, 87, 99, 109). In these poems Copley exhibits an effective simplicity of language and a scholar's grasp of tone and meaning; they, together with the sober introduction and notes, might serve as the core of a revised edition which would jettison the mannerisms and vulgarity[16] which so mar the present translation.

[Other opinion. A. Dalzell (*Phoenix* 12 [1958] 193f.)

expressed strong reservations about Copley's use of low language, but called his edition 'a vigorous Catullus and a complete Catullus'.]

✠ THE POEMS OF CATULLUS, transl. Peter Whigham. Harmondsworth (Middlesex): Penguin Books 1966. Pp. 246; $1.25 paper. Also available in a bilingual edition published by University of California Press 1968, $7.50 cloth.
Predominantly free verse; formal metre used for special effect (heroic couplets in 66, ia^5 in 76). The introduction (13-46) discursively treats Catullus's life, his relationship with Lesbia (= Clodia Metelli, p. 15f.), his literary circle (pp. 24-29, the best section), and the long poems 61-68. There is a glossary (pp. 229-246).

Whigham's procedure is almost the antithesis of Mills's: 'I have taken different readings from different texts, and different suggestions from different scholars. . .and having selected my material on the basis of what I found most stimulating poetically, I have then tried to rewrite the poem as I imagined Catullus might have written it had he been alive today and writing in English. As a poem is more than the sum of its constituent parts, a certain ruthlessness over details is often necessary.' Close translation is hardly to be expected from one with such beliefs, nor is sober interpretation to be looked for from one who acknowledges Robinson Ellis as his chief guide in text and exegesis. Whigham's 'rewriting' at times makes the original unrecognisable (e.g., 51); one is also uncertain whether what look like mistranslations are the howlers they seem or part of the method, e.g., 50.18f. *precesque nostras,/oramus, cave ne despuas, ocelle* 'don't/look peremptory, or/contemn my apple'. Whigham should not be given to students as 'Catullus' (*expertus dico*!), but he should be read by all familiar with the Latin for his not infrequent gems of translation (most of them in the witty poems, e.g., 17, 22, 42, 67; but note also 65, 109).

[Other opinion. K.F.C. Rose (*CW* 60 [1967] 394) called

Whigham's translation 'a splendid achievement', and S. Commager (*New York Times Book Review*, August 15, 1971, 35) called his schemes 'possibly more exciting' than those of Michie.]

⁂ CATULLUS, transl. C.H. Sisson. London: MacGibbon and Kee 1966. Pp. 93; £1.25 cloth.
Free verse. This edition, with its tall pages, its white cover and gold lettering, and its freedom from the clutter of introduction or notes, resembles the proverbial 'slim volume of poems'. The impression is not misleading, for Sisson is a poet rather than a scholar, as is obvious from his three-page 'postscript' on Catullus's place in Latin literature. Traces of his amateur status also emerge in his dependence on the Loeb text (to the extent of omitting 16.7-14) and in the many mistranslations that disfigure his pages.

Some examples: 31.11 *hoc est quod unum est pro laboribus tantis* 'this is really all we undertake these toils for'; 46.4 *linquantur Phrygii, Catulle, campi* 'Catullus, now they leave the Phrygian plains'; 68.128 *(improbius) quam quae praecipue multivola est mulier* 'though women are notably inconstant'; 84.5 *liber avunculus eius* 'his uncle Liber'.

Although Sisson has a number of clear successes (13, 41, 43, 53, 70, 76, 83, 86, 87, 96, 99, 101), and although he is, of all Catullus's translators, the least daunted by *versiculi parum pudici*, his frequent lapses on the lowest level of translation make it impossible to commend him for our purposes.

[Other opinion. J.J. Bateman (*CW* 61 [1968] 254-255): 'Sisson dulls the language and imagery to banality. . .but. . .he is usually true to the literal meaning and does not indulge his fancy'; E.R.A. Sewter (*G and R* 14 [1967] 190): 'it must be admitted that he is eminently successful with Catullus's obscenities'.]

⁂ THE POEMS OF CATULLUS, transl. Horace Gregory. New York: Grove Press 1956. Pp. xxiv, 184; $1.95 paper.
Free verse; in 11 and 51 an approximation of the sapphic

stanza is used. The introduction (pp. v-xxiv) is largely autobiographical, but also includes unreliable information about Catullus's life and the transmission of his poetry. There is one page of notes, in which the poems are called by the uncommon name 'stanzas' (sample comment: '51st stanza—There have been many arguments over the disposition of the fourth stanza. The first three stanzas are part of the famous translation of Sappho. The last stanza is Catullus's own').

Although this version has apparently attracted readers for many years (p. xxiii), it cannot be recommended. Gregory has a compulsion to embroider the text with his own images and to spell out what he thinks is the meaning of a lein, rather than rendering the exact degree of explicitness of the Latin. Failure to grasp a poem's hypothesis is thus evident in the translation (as in 42, seen as a military call to arms), and even more frequently Catullus's ideas are replaced by inferior ones: e.g., 31.1f. 'O my little almost island, little island Sirmio,/this brave eye, this bright green jewel set in Neptune's fair estate/of lucid waters and broad seas';[17] 51.10f. 'ears resound with noise of distant storms shaking/this earth, eyes gaze on stars that fall forever/into deep midnight'. This tendency, added to Gregory's looseness of form, involves him in difficulties in a complex structure, such as 68, where at several points his version calls his understanding of the text into question: from lines 68f. ('then you lead the way/into a house and to its mistress where all could follow the/demands of love! there where I found my lady...') one gets a novel and disturbing impression of Allius's service to Catullus; other surprises are that Protesilaus's death was demanded by the gods as a blood-sacrifice to purify his own house, that Hercules killed the Stymphalian birds inside the drainage-channel of Pheneus, and that the welcome child of lines 119f. is the offspring of Laodamia and Protesilaus.

Despite his publisher's reputation, Gregory is perhaps the most prudish modern translator of Catullus: 16.1 is rendered 'Furius, Aurelius, I'll work your own perversions/upon you and your persons'; the reprise of the opening line appears as 'I'll be ready/to defile you and seduce you'.

✠ CATULLUS: THE COMPLETE POEMS FOR AMERICAN READERS, transl. Reney Myers and Robert J. Ormsby. New York: Dutton 1970. Pp. xviii, 190; $2.25 paper.

Bilingual edition; various metrical schemes, all with rhyme. Quincy Howe's introduction is an extreme example of the biographical fallacy; the remarks on Catullus and the *neoteroi* and on the survival of Catullus are less accurate than those available in other editions. The glossary is incomplete; with the curious exceptions 'pumice stone' and 'radishes and fish', it contains only proper names.

This most recent translation is also nearly the worst version of Catullus now in print. Its critical defect springs from the decision to use, for the short poems, rhyme-schemes similar to those of the English sonnet (e.g., abba cddc etc., with many variations), often in conjunction with a short line, such as the ia^4. Manipulation of such a tight structure requires a skill in the use of English which the translators do not have; the result is the loss or distortion of Catullus's ideas and their replacement by matter invented for the sake of rhyme. The process is endemic, at best producing an approximation of the original, as in 34.1f. 'In Diana's care,/ good girls and boys, we sing/of Diana, pure and fair,/in our caroling', at worst resulting in drivel, often with no relation or even an opposite relation to Catullus's meaning: e.g., 34.23f. 'give/your help to Romulus' heirs/so all, like him, may live'; 68.160 'more precious to me than my life and art'; 86.6 'she's captured all the graces: these I sing'. I am rather at a loss to explain the subtitle of this edition, since the translators often favour a literary style remote from the rhythms of American, or any other, speech, e.g. 8.3f. 'But once bright, golden suns beamed down and cast/a happiness on you'; 9f. 'Yet now she does not love you, and alas,/you must not chase her nor live wretchedly,/thus make your heart as hard as it can be'; perhaps 'American readers' are expected to react with pleased recognition to the indiscriminate coarseness with which the translators render Catullus's varied and picturesque obscenity (e.g., 15.19, 28.9f., 33.4, 39.21, 58.5, etc.) and which they frequently insert with no support at all from the text (e.g., 25.5, 37.20, 39.21, 41.4, 8; 42.11, 20; 57.9). It is perhaps a good thing that this edition includes a Latin text; too often there is little of Catullus on the opposite pages.

[Other opinion. D.P. Harmon (*CW* 64 [1970/71] 203), while expressing reservations about some of the rhymes and the unnecessary use of obscene language, calls the translations 'charming, witty, and daring. . .a fascinating addition to the study of Catullus'.]

❧ CATULLUS transl. Celia and Louis Zukofsky. London: Cape Groliard Press 1969 (U.S. distribution in collaboration with Grossman Publishers, New York). Pp. unnumbered; $4.50 paper, $9.50 cloth.

Bilingual edition. I cite *in toto* the translators' explanation of their technique: 'This translation of Catullus follows the sound, rhythm, and syntax of his Latin—tries, as is said, to breathe the "literal" meaning with him'. The aim, less than lucidly explained in these words, is to render Catullus's Latin in English which, first of all, sounds like it and, *longo sed proximus intervallo*, which means something like it. Little thought is needed to see that the plan is quite mad; rigorously applied, it produces gibberish (e.g., 46.2f. *nam te esse Tiburtem autumant, quibus non est/cordi Catullum laedere; at quibus cordist,/quovis Sabinum pignore esse contendunt* 'now addressed Tiburtine it means the wish, *no nest/accord Catullus more, love there;* quibbles core dust,/so pig who pins Sabine on him—ass, contendent' [the italics are the translators']). Faint hope is held out by the early poems (2, 3, 5, 7), in which the Method is only intermittently present (7 is spoiled only by 'sidereal moult' for *sidera multa*), but the translators are finally overcome by their own folly. What causes regret is that Louis Zukofsky is capable of the best sort of poetic translation; for the space of single phrases he can even bring off his crazy scheme (e.g., 8.1 *miser Catulle* 'miss her, Catullus? ., 13.1 *cenabis* 'canapés'), and many of these versions are studded with exciting recreations (e.g., 11.17f. 'in the moist/clasp (cp. *moechis/quos*) of one concourse of three hundred lechers'; 16.6 'his versicles not nailed to his need'). Anyone familiar with Catullus should glance at this edition to see what Zukofsky might have produced, but I do not urge anyone to buy the book; *afficionados* of this type of literary activity will be more consistently pleased by the recent volume *Mots d'Heures, Gousses, Rames,* by L.van Rooten (New York: Grossman 1967, $3.95), which has the added attraction of a suitable commentary and which does not masquerade as a translation of a great poet.

[Other opinion. S. Commager (*New York Times Book Review*, August 15, 1971, 35): 'The offspring of the Zukofskys' joint attempt is unique. One may hope that it remains so'; see also the full discussion by B. Raffel, *Arion* 8.3 (1969) 435-445.]

HORACE

THE ODES AND EPODES OF HORACE. A MODERN ENGLISH VERSE TRANSLATION, transl. Joseph P. Clancy. Chicago: University of Chicago Press 1960. Pp. 257; $1.95 paper.
No strict metre or rhyme, but the general shape of Horace's metres is preserved. The introduction gives, in addition to the usual biographical material, an uncommonly detailed account of the problems involved in translating Horace and a select bibliography; each of the three sections of the book (*Odes* I-III; *Odes* IV; *Epodes*) has its own introductory note, dealing with the arrangement and character of the poems and discussing a few in some detail. There are brief notes and a full glossary.

THE ODES OF HORACE, transl. James Michie. New York: Washington Square Press 1965. Pp. xx, 286; $0.90 paper; also available, with the addition of the *Carmen Saeculare*, as no. 202 of the Bobbs-Merrill Library of Liberal Arts series (Indianapolis 1965, $1.95 paper).
Bilingual edition. Thirteen poems (eleven of them Alcaics) are rendered into the original metres; elsewhere a stanza of four to six lines unified by rhyme is the most common form. Rex Warner's introduction attempts to defend Horace from the charge of 'insincerity' (ix-xiv); Michie gives a quick but thoughtful sketch of Horace's life and personality (xv-xx). The notes and glossary are by J. Coates: the notes are fuller than Clancy's, the glossary less so.

These two editions are both of high quality, and are also in a sense complementary. The skill in handling strict metrical structures which distinguished Michie's Catullus is even more on display here, though it produces unevenly impressive results; the extreme pressure to which Horace subjects his material comes across, but his particular methods (word-order, juxtaposition, etc.) are inimitable. It cannot surprise that such an ambitious programme is not entirely successful: for some poems the choice of metre is wrong (the fourth Archilochian of 1.4 fails, rhymed couplets are too light for 1.24), and there are many places where Michie strains or distorts to achieve his effects (e.g., 1.37 last lines: 'was she to grace a haughty triumph?. . .Not Cleopatra!'; 3.13.6f. 'the hot goat people's son/must wish his crimson one/dye your cool vein'; 4.13.7 'Chia's soft cheeks, whose youth and lyre/know how to rouse desire'). But on the whole his versions inspire admiration.

Clancy has chosen another, less demanding approach, and has succeeded within the limits set by that decision. His looser structure allows him to stay much closer to Horace's literal meaning and also his form: he preserves Horace's stanza divisions, while Michie must often add one or more of his shorter stanzas in the course of a poem. His language is unobstrusively modern, and he is generally good at indicating Horace's variations of tone (although lapses do reveal themselves: e.g., 1.4.7 'lightly to waltz in the grass' is the opposite of *quatiunt terram*; 1.9.21 *proditor risus* 'giveaway giggles'). His most serious flaw is an occasional misplaced flat or prosaic phrase: e.g., 2.16.28 'nothing is wholly/filled with happiness'; 3.6.13f. 'in the grip of civil conflicts the city/was nearly wiped out by Egypt and Dacia'; 4.5.32 'in due course' (*alteris mensis*); but these are outnumbered by many resourceful renderings of individual phrases and lines (several times duplicated by Michie). Choosing between these editions will be a matter of taste: Clancy may be thought more reliable, Michie more exciting. Price may not be irrelevant: the Washington Square edition of Michie, despite its bilious jacket-design, is clearly a 'best buy'.

[Other opinion. *Clancy*: J. Crossett (*CJ* 56 [1960/61] 187-188): 'the good outweighs the bad and the successes are very good indeed'. *Michie*: L.P. Wilkinson (*CR* N.S. 15 [1965] 358-359: 'alive and agreeable to read'; M.L. Lee (*Phoenix* 20 [1966] 92) was in general approving, but found certain rhymes questionable.]

❦ THE ODES OF HORACE. NEWLY TRANSLATED FROM THE LATIN AND RENDERED INTO THE ORIGINAL METRES, transl. Helen Rowe Henze. Norman (Okla.): University of Oklahoma Press 1961. Pp. xiii, 229; $5.95 cloth.

The introduction, indebted to Alfred Noyes, is biographical rather than critical. An appendix contains metrical schemata, and there is both a glossary and pronunciation guide to proper names.

Whether Horace's metres can be successfully duplicated in English is doubtful; *this* attempt, at least, the first to render the corpus of *Odes*, does not come off. The padding and repetition Henze introduces destroy Horace's economy of words and images.

E.g., 1.9.18f. 'Now 'neath the *falling* dusk, at the trysting hour/*again, again* through field and courtyard/let the soft whispers be *still* repeated (=*repetantur!*); 1.23.11f. 'leave your mother, *my dear child...*'; 2.10.13f. 'still the heart, the well-prepared heart'.

Horace's sharpness is further blurred by not infrequent doubtful or wrong translations.

E.g., 1.1.1 'Maecenas, from your royal sires *so lately* sprung'; 1.9.14 'and what the day shall bring, what of chance (=*Fors*?) or gain (*lucro*?), set down to profit'; 1.8.15f. *ne virilis/cultus in caedem et Lycias proriperet catervas* 'lest a man's garb and lest the/Lycian allies hasten him forth'.

It is an annoyance to the reader that every poem should be spotted with footnotes which merely identify the metre and proper names, information which should be relegated to the appendix and glossary.

[Other opinion. J.M. Benario (*CJ* 58 [1961/62] 84-85) felt that 'diction and poetic grace have...suffered' from Henze's concern with metre.]

MARTIAL

MARTIAL: SELECTED EPIGRAMS, transl. Rolfe Humphries. Bloomington (Ind.): Indiana University Press 1963. Pp. 127; $1.95 paper.

About 150 items; rhymed couplets or shorter lines (ia^4, tr^4), but with a sizeable minority of the elegiacs and hendecasyllables rendered into the original metre. Palmer Bovie's introduction (pp. 7-23) perhaps unwisely presses the parallels between Flavian Rome and the London of Johnson, Pope, and Swift; his notes gloss the translator's modern allusions (e.g., Katisha, haggis, Ben-Hur) as well as those which stem from Martial.

MARTIAL: SELECTED EPIGRAMS, transl. Ralph Marcellino. Indianapolis: Bobbs-Merrill (Library of Liberal Arts no. 127) 1968. Pp. xii, 160; $2.25 paper.

Rhymed stanzas of two or four lines (xaxa the most common form); 150 items. A short preface contains a life of Martial; there is a select bibliography (only one item out of twenty-three is wholly concerned with Martial and is not an edition or translation), and a section of notes (pp. 155-160).

EPIGRAMS FROM MARTIAL, transl. Barriss Mills. Lafayette (Ind.): Purdue University Press 1969. Pp. xx, 200; $6.95 cloth.

About 400 items; free verse. The introduction (pp. ix-xvii) contains useful remarks on Martial's *persona*, although the previous development of the epigram is seriously misrepresented ('the epigram, as Martial inherited it from earlier poets, was a rather formless, indeterminate literary genre', p. xi). No notes or glossary.

Translators of Martial are inevitably afflicted with their author's *inaequalitas*. Careful selection and skilful handling can only hope to be rewarded by a verdict the reverse of Martial's own: *sunt mala, sunt quaedam mediocria, sunt bona plura/quae legis hic.*

The three translations described above differ both in the selection they present and the techniques they employ. Each can record at least some successes *vis-à-vis* its rivals; none is wholly satisfactory. Mills offers easily the largest selection, more than a quarter of Martial's output. His versions are close and plain, and at times this gives him the advantage over more flashy translators (e.g., 1.10, 28; 3.9; 4.89; 10.8, 40, 48; 11.62, 66), but his literal approach becomes a drawback when it prevents him from re-arranging a poem's elements for better effect in English or adding words for needed emphasis; the result is correct, but lifeless (e.g., 1.57, 73; 8.69; 9.53, 70; 10.62, 91; 12.7). Mills is best at the longer poems, where the effect is less concentrated; these poems are given less attention by other translators (*quibus breviora, non meliora placent*), and Mills's edition is a useful corrective to the common picture of Martial as a two-line comic.

Both Humphries and Marcellino have the advantage of metre and rhyme, almost a necessity for an effective English epigram, and both have successes which depend on the clinching power of the metrical form (Humphries 2.9, 80, 87; 3.9; 5.9; 6.23; 10.91; Marcellino 2.42; 9.88; 10.43; 14.175). Humphries is, however, by far the more skilful versifier; too often Marcellino gropes for a rhyme (in 10.62 and 12.20 the exclamation 'hell' is mere filler) or produces verses inspired by Hallmark rather than Martial (e.g., 12.34.3f. 'though joys were mixed with sorrows/that tried our friendships sore,/yet weighed against each other, sure/the joys were rather more'). To be set against this is Humphries's greater inaccuracy, both in details (e.g., 2.11.4 *quod paene terram nasus indecens tangit* 'his ugly chin upon his chest is laid'; 3.49.1 the distinction between *misces* and *potas* is missed) and in more substantial things (1.16.1 *quaedam mediocria, mala plura* ‘some so-so, some bad’; in 3.25 it is Sabinus’s oratory, not his ‘disposition’, that has power to freeze the *thermae*). On balance Mills is the most accurate of these translators, Humphries the most enjoyable.

⁂ EPIGRAMS OF MARTIAL, transl. Palmer Bovie. New York: New American Library (Plume Books) 1970. Pp. 207; $3.95 paper.
Free verse, with occasional rhyme in couplets; 451 items (*Liber Spectaculorum* and books I-IV complete, with selections from the other books in the interstices). The introduction (pp. 9-24) offers more description than analysis of Martial’s poetry, and gives disproportionate attention to the minor *Liber Spectaculorum* and the unrepresented books of *Xenia* and *Apophoreta* (pp. 12-19). There are sketchy notes (pp. 199-205) and a ‘bibliographical note’ (p. 207).

It was an excellent plan to offer several books of Martial complete, showing the poet in all his variety and unevenness, but the translations themselves are not entirely equal to the task. Bovie lacks a distinctive tone of voice—he has neither Mills’s literalness nor the inventive originality of Humphries—and his form is so loose as to seem shapeless. He scores some successes (e.g., 1.27, 110; 3.2, 28, 32-33, 65, 70, 92, 100), but yields too often to flat, padded, or approximate renderings, e.g., 1.10.3 ‘what attracts him so is her ominous racking cough’; 1.30 ‘Doctor Diaulus who started as a surgeon/has gone on to become an undertaker/so his bedside manner is still urgent’; 5.34.9f. ‘Oh green earth, rest lightly on her! Do not/bear down too hard on her there, who was/never a trouble or a burden to you, here’ (also 1.112, 2.78, 3.8, 9, 21, 26.6, 27.4). Further, the percentage of error is too high; more than a few epigrams are demolished or weakened by mistranslation.

E.g., 2.87 *dicis amore tui bellas ardere puellas* ‘the girls burn with love, for Sextus they simmer’; 7.89.4 *sic te semper amet Venus* ‘so, you will requite/your loving Venus' prayer'; 10.47.13 *summum nec metuas diem nec optes* 'If you live like this, my good friend Julius Martial,/you won't either long for/or wince at/your last day on earth'; 3.15.2 *'Cum sit tam pauper, quomodo?' Caecus amat* 'And yet he's poor? He has a consuming interest in Caecus' (note also 3.12.4, 3.6.5f., 3.13.2, 3.30.5f., 3.69.5f., 3.78, 3.84).

The following are not worth serious consideration:

Sixty Poems of Martial in Translation, transl. Dudley Fitts. New York: Harcourt, Brace 1956. Pp. xiii, 127; $4.95 cloth. Bilingual edition; free verse. Short preface (pp. ix-x) and index of Latin first lines.

The selection is neither comprehensive nor generous—almost all the poems chosen are what Fitts terms 'destructive' epigrams, and nearly five-sixths contain four or fewer lines. The renderings are self-indulgent and loose, but even so the level of original wit displayed is too often sophomoric (the only amusing turn I noted is in 3.53: 'Take oh take that face away...'). The work was clearly a parergon, and its lavish publication inevitably prompts the question '*aes dabo pro nugis et emam tua carmina sanus?*'.

Poems After Martial, by Philip Murray. Middletown (Conn.): Wesleyan University Press 1963. Pp. ix, 87; $4.50 cloth. Various metres; about seventy items. The introduction (pp. 3-11) discusses earlier translations of Martial. The title is apt; the originals are seldom entirely lost from view, but few of these versions are straight translations. The selection is weighted in favour of the wittily insulting; a notable feature in this late season is the frequent bowdlerisation (e.g., 3.82, 7.58, 9.37, 11.21, 66). The comparisons Murray makes in the introduction between his own and other translations are revealing, but do not always work in his favour.

[Other opinion. *Humphries*: W.S. Anderson (*CW* 57 [1964] 381), 'I recommend the translations, not the notes'; D. Henry and B. Walker (*CP* 60 [1965] 215-19) criticised the anachronisms; A. Ker (*CR* N.S. 15 [1965] 121) approved of the shorter epigrams, but noted a tendency to add to the original;

G. Roberts (*CJ* 60 [1965] 236), 'he has generally been successful–sometimes astonishingly so'. *Marcellino:* W.S. Anderson (*CW* 62 [1968] 141-142) criticised a tendency to pad; E.R.A. Sewter (*G and R* 15 [1968] 200), 'the notes are minimal, but the versions are excellent'. *Fitts, Marcellino, Murray:* W.S. Anderson (*CW* 62 [1968] 141-142), 'In general both Murray and Marcellino can be safely recommended to the classicist, for pleasure and edification. Fitts, I feel, was not working very hard when he put together this volume'.]

OVID, AMORES

LOVE POEMS OF OVID (contains *Amores* 1.2-5, 7-10, 13, 14; 2.2-4, 6-8, 11, 12, 15, 19; 3.2, 3, 5, 10, and selections from the *Ars Amatoria* (pp. 99-116) and the *Remedia Amoris* (pp. 119-126), transl. Horace Gregory. New York: New American Library 1964. Pp. 126; $0.75 paper.
Free verse. The introduction (pp. ix-xviii) is unreliable on Ovid's life and background; the comparison made between the *Amores* and Herrick's *Hesperides* is interesting, that with Colette's novels much less so. No notes or glossary.

Gregory has aimed at re-creating Ovid's 'immediacy, lightness, spontaneity, and polish' (p. xviii), but the result cannot be said to succeed. His versions are too often verbose, graceless, and seriously inaccurate.

Their besetting fault is wordiness: e.g., 1.3.1 *iusta precor* 'I swear I do not ask too much of heaven'; 1.5.2 *medio toro* 'where the couch sank to embrace me'; 1.5.24 *requievimus* 'we had a brief, but deep siesta'. New ideas are often added to or substituted for Ovid's: e.g., 1.3.1f. *quae me nuper praedata puella est/aut amet aut faciat cur ego semper amem* 'O make that thoughtless girl/who yesterday made me her spoils of war either love me/or let me share her bed to prove I love her'[18], 1.3.15f. *non mihi mille placent, non sum desultor amoris: tu mihi, si qua fides, cura perennis eris* 'A thousand women hold no interest for me./One in a thousand/shall be the girl I love. Love makes me faithful'. In the process Ovid's sharply observed images are sometimes lost; e.g., 1.9.11f. *duplicataque nimbo/flumina* 'great rivers that spread round him in a flood of rain'; 1.9.41 *discinctaque in otia* 'at ease, in country quiet'. Often the rendering is so approximate that one suspects the meaning of the Latin has been missed, e.g., 1.3.8f. *si nostri sanguinis auctor eques,/nec meus innumeris renovatur campus aratris* 'the first Naso [!] was of lesser gentry—/he rode his horse and ran a small plantation'; 1.3.13 *nulli cessura fides* 'unlike most men, I always keep my word'.

In short, the filter through which Ovid's poetry must pass

in this translation removes too much of its style and substance.

⁂ THE ART OF LOVE (*Amores, Ars Amatoria, Medicamina Faciei Feminei, Remedia Amoria*), transl. Rolfe Humphries. Bloomington (Ind.): Indiana University Press 1957. Pp. 206; $1.95 paper.
Approximation of original metre in most poems (though the pentameters are sometimes catalectic hexameters, and the form of the second half is _oo_oo_); others are rendered by sonnets or multiples of sonnets. The short preface does something to situate the *Amores* within Ovid's production, but does not place them in any wider context. No notes or glossary.

These translations are fatally handicapped by their metre. The English hexameter is an inelegant form, and the English pentameter is hardly better. To produce the verse-endings _oo_x and _oo x, English must resort to stilted or lame combinations of noun plus possessive phrase, e.g., 'sight of a lion', 'lap of her judge'; in one poem of fifty-two verses (*Am.* 1.2), twelve such combinations appear. Further, the padding required by the English hexameter gives rise to some puzzling expressions, e.g., *Am.* 1.6.36 *ante vel a membris dividar ipse meis* 'that would tear from my side part of my actual self'; 1.13.3f. *sic Memnonis umbris/annua sollemni caede parentet avis* 'wait while the starlings of Memnon/pay their annual rite, dark in the shadows of air'. Finally, the translations are alarmingly cavalier in omitting or compressing Ovid's material and replacing it with original ideas; the tendency is especially pronounced in the sonnet-metre versions, e.g., *Am.* 1.5.

⁂ OVID'S AMORES, transl. Guy Lee. London: John Murray, New York: Viking 1968. Pp. vii, 202; £0.80, $1.65 paper, £1.50, $5.75 cloth.
Bilingual edition; free verse. Notes (pp. 181-194) give mythological details, explicate literary allusions and borrowings,

and discuss important textual uncertainties. A highly satisfactory life of Ovid (pp. 195-198) and a note on the translation (pp. 199-201) close the book.

This is an exciting and provocative translation, and it should be said immediately that it is the best modern translation of these poems. The author is a Cambridge Ovidian, and his thorough understanding of the text is apparent; his scholarship is accurate and up-to-date, and one only regrets that the notes in which it is imparted are not more numerous.[19] The versions themselves are fresh, laced with dry wit, and a pleasure to read.

Their form and style, however, are somewhat controversial. Lee eschews metre and rhyme, and strives for the utmost leanness of language. As an illustration of the process consider the translation of 1.6.69f.: *tu dominae, cum te proiectam mane videbit,/temporis absumpti tam male testis eris* 'My love will see it lying there/in token of a wasted night'. To balance the need in English for many unimportant particles, full advantage is taken of places where English expresses an idea more succinctly than Latin ('wasted' = *absumpti tam male*), and Latin words are omitted when their force can be found in the context (e.g., *mane*). The absence of formal metre in such formal poems as the *Amores* must be felt as a lack, but it is mitigated by Lee's respect for the couplet (heightened by typographical spacing) and compensated for by the intensity of expression his streamlined diction makes possible.

Lee compares his method with its opposite, the inflation English must undergo to be turned into idiomatic Latin, and challenges scholars to turn his English back into Ovidian elegiacs before concluding that it is too free. By this criterion some renderings do lose their apparent boldness: e.g., 1.5.23f. *singula quid referam? nil non laudabile vidi,/et nudam pressi corpus ad usque meum* 'why list perfection?/I hugged her tight'; 1.11.8 *et obstantes sedula pelle moras* 'immediately'. Passages remain, however, in which Ovid's *color* is untranslated: e.g., 1.3.22 *et quam fluminea lusit adulter ave* 'Leda who loved a swan' (where 'Leda deceived by a swan' would be closer); 1.6.72 *lente nec admisso turpis amante* 'you oafish locker-out of lovers'; and others in which a *color* is rendered by an inexact equivalent, e.g., 1.6.74 *duraque conservae ligna, valete fores* 'wooden door/goodbye—and thanks for your servility'; 3.2.8 *ergo illi curae contigit esse tuae* 'He's a lucky man to be picked by you'. But such flaws are venial; the wit of the poems generally remains intact. The edition deserves a wide audience; a bibliography would be a welcome addition.

[Other opinion. *Gregory:* W.T. Avery (*CW* 58 [1964] 22) found these versions prurient and salacious, and recommended them warmly. *Lee:* M.V. Cunningham (*CW* 62 [1968] 105) praised the translations as smooth, clear, and competent, and noted the scholarly qualities of the edition.]

PROPERTIUS

THE POEMS OF PROPERTIUS, transl. Constance Carrier. Bloomington (Ind.): Indiana University Press 1963. Pp. 224; $1.95 paper
Loose ia^5 with alternating rhyme (i.e., xaxa xbxb etc.). Palmer Bovie's introduction (pp. 9-22) dwells on Propertius's effect on Goethe and Pound, and is impressionistic rather than factual in approach. The notes (pp. 195-200) are often mere references to the glossary (pp. 201-224). There is an ill-assorted bibliography (p. 195).

THE POEMS OF PROPERTIUS, transl. A.E. Watts, Harmondsworth (Middlesex): Penguin Books 1966. Pp. 236; $1.45 paper.
Rhymed couplets (ia^5). The wide-ranging introduction (pp. 7-36) discusses the 'dramatic' character of Propertius's poetry and its use of mythology; informed and up-to-date suggestions for further reading are given. There are no notes, but the exhaustive glossary (pp. 199-236) explicates many obscure references.

To translate Propertius at all is an act of daring; to translate him into the most restrictive of English verse-forms, the heroic couplet, verges on foolhardiness. Yet Watts carries off this feat with a skill that commands admiration and in most cases compels conviction. The technical aspect of his achievement may be described in words a better critic once applied to a less fortunate translator of Propertius: 'the rendering is close and deft, the English is pure, the phrasing neat, the lines run well'. Equally impressive, however, is Watts's retention of the Propertian manner: almost all his genuine difficulty is there, the allusive mythology, the unexpected transitions, the idiosyncratic phrases[20]; these couplets sound Ovidian only when Propertius indulges in 'Ovidian' point (e.g., 4.4.57f.). Such an undertaking must have its flaws. Sometimes the pull of the metrical form is responsible, but other renderings are dubious or simply wrong.

Need for a rhyme to 'Callimachus' in 3.1.2 calls forth the cliché 'deathless genius'; desire to preserve the climactic position of *Iovis* in 2.13.16 shrinks the grand *inimicitias* to the wan 'frown' and inflates *tunc* to 'thus favoured'; the compression of 4.11.43f. ('bear witness that undimmed the glories shone/of your great house in me, its paragon') ignores the movement from *non dammum* (via *quin!*) to *pars imitanda.*

In 1.3.24f. the words *cavis manibus* are referred to Propertius, the phrase *munera de prono saepe voluta sinu* to Cynthia[21]; in 1.16.33 *nunc iacet alterius felici nixa lacerto* means 'now she lies propped up by another man's lucky arm', not 'now blessing someone's arms, she nestles there'.

There are others, but they are few; no more than might be found in many scholarly discussions of the poet. All in all, this is a successful piece of work.

Carrier has in a sense aimed lower, since her metrical structure is far more accommodating, but even so her translation is seriously deficient. It is unfaithful to the letter of the text in several ways, none of which serve the spirit. Paraphrase is used not only to give the gist of a corrupt or uncertain passage, but also to evade the mythological allusions that form a staple element of Roman poetic sensibility; a defensible procedure, but not when the result is lameness.

2.10.13f. *iam negat Euphrates equitem post terga tueri/Parthorum et Crassos se tenuisse dolet* 'Now Parthia must mourn the Parthian shot,/ and Crassus's death, and Parthia's role in it'; 2.13.8 *tunc ego sim Inachio notior arte Lino* 'and I may reap more fame than the greatest could'; also 3.13.9f., 4.7.22, 1.1.9f., 1.3.24f., 41f., 2.10.4f., 25f.[22]

More disturbing is the simple omission of significant words or even of entire phrases or lines, balanced by the insertion of non-Propertian touches.

E.g., 1.3.25f., 34, 46; 1.16.45-46; 1.22.3 si. . .tibi sunt nota, 7 mei. . . *propinqui;* 2.13.36 *servus;* 3.1.17 *quod pace legas;* 4.11.79 *illis,* 86 *cauta.*

1.3.10 *et quaterent sera nocte facem pueri* 'the dying light/of the slaves' torches lit the dying night'; 1.16.15 'the faithful lover, who is here/perpetually, a taint, a leech, a curse'; 2.10.18 *sentiat illa tuas postmodo capta manus* 'will feel his hand, mighty in peace and war'.

Finally, there are numerous doubtful interpretations and mistranslations.

The first thirty lines of 4.7 alone yield the following: 6 *et quererer lecti frigida regna mei* 'in the bed that was once our kingdom and was no more'; 7 *eosdem habuit secum quibus est elata capillos* 'her eyes, her hair, were the same as I had known them'; 13 *perfide nec cuiquam melior sperande puellae* 'you forget so soon...no woman ever had a truer lover'; 26 *laesit* 'props up'; 27 *quis nostro curvum te funere vidit?* 'who has seen you stand by my grave grief-stricken?';[23] 29 *si piguit portas ultra procedere* 'if you could not bear to pass beyond my doorway';[23] *illuc* 'here'.

It is unfair to ask a reader to give up so much of Propertius and to receive so little in return.

THE POEMS OF PROPERTIUS, transl. John Warden. Indianapolis: Bobbs-Merrill 1972 (Library of Liberal Arts 166). Pp. xiv, 269; $8.50 cloth, $2.95 paper.

Mainly free verse, but with formal metre used for special effects (e.g., *terza rima* in 1.16.1-16, 45-48; rhymed couplets in 3.13, etc.) A foreword deliberately does no more than hint at the character of Propertius's poetry; there is a useful and up-to-date bibliography, a short but adequate life of Propertius, and a 'note on the text' which acknowledges the edition of Camps as the primary guide in matters of text and interpretation.[24] There are no notes, but there is a glossary (pp. 233-269) which compares well, in size and usefulness, with that of Watts.

Professor Warden's Propertius has much to recommend it, not least its freedom from eccentricity. It is generally accurate[25] and therefore preferable to Carrier, and its loose metrical form avoids the quaintness which Watt's rhymed couplets do not always escape. In this translation Propertius speaks an unobtrusively but unmistakeably modern form of English in which the rhythms of real speech can often be made out.

This virtue, however, has its less attractive side, a lowering of both poetic and emotional tension. Several aspects of the translator's approach contribute to an unfortunate impression of cool discursiveness, at times verging on flaccidity. Emotional words are rendered by neutral expressions (so in 1.1.7 *furor hic* becomes 'this restless passion', and in 1.1.38 *heu quanto...dolore* 'with sorrow') or omitted completely (2. 13.25 *sat mea sat magna est*). Rhetorical points are often blunted (3.13.20 *pudor est non licuisse mori* 'not to live in shame'; 21 *ardent victrices* untranslated; also 1.16.47-48, 4.11.60). Allusive phrases are occasionally interpreted in the translation;[26] the result is clear, but flat (1.1.12 *Hylaei percussus vulnere rami* 'he tackled the lecherous centaur and felt the weight of his club'; 27 *ferrum saevos...et ignis* 'the pain of the surgeon's knife and the savage burning'). At other times the Latin is expanded for no apparent reason (1.3.2 *languida* 'a picture of peace'; 17 *dominae turbare quietem* 'disturb her when she looked so quiet and peaceful'; 2.13.11 *me iuvet in gremio doctae legisse puellae* 'a girl with the wit to listen to my songs of love/as she holds me in her arms; 4.11.35 *iungor, Paulle, tuo sic discessura cubili* 'I gave myself, then, Paullus, to your couch,/and nothing could make me leave it, nothing but death'). A recurrent technique in the process of expansion is hendiadys, by which a complex Latin phrase is unpacked into two simple, paratactically arranged English phrases (e.g. 1.1.1 *Cynthia prima suis miserum me cepit ocellis* 'CYNTHIA. She was the first to enslave me, and she did it with her eyes'; 4.11.73 *tibi commendo communia pignora natos* 'I give the children to your care,/the pledges of the love we shared together').

Although the foregoing comments may suggest that Professor Warden has not been entirely successful in capturing the spirit of Propertius in English, the character of the competing versions makes it almost certain that his translation will be widely used in the immediate future.

[Other opinion. *Carrier:* R.J. Hebein (*CB* 42 [1966] 93) called this version 'as accurate as a verse rendering can be expected to be'; D. Henry and B. Walker (*CP* 60 [1965] 215f.) found it padded. *Watts:* W.A. Camps (*CR* N.S. 13 [1963] 224) found 'limitations and very real merits' in this version, but noted that 'the style adopted seems. . .to be more appropriate to Ovid than to Propertius'.]

TIBULLUS

THE POEMS OF TIBULLUS, transl. Constance Carrier. Bloomington (Ind.): Indiana University Press 1968. Pp. 128; $1.95 paper, $5.75 cloth.
Lines of three, five, or six stresses *κατὰ στίχον*, the last at times with alternating rhyme (xaxa xbxb etc.). Edward M. Michael's introduction (pp. 7-31) is a serious essay on Tibullus's poetry, discussing themes and techniques and treating some poems in detail. It is not free of cant ('protactic function', 'paraphiliac expedient', 'ring-composition'), and its literal-minded interpretation of Tibullus's love-affairs with 'Delia', 'Nemesis', and 'Marathus' may be thought misguided. The numbered notes are grouped at the back (pp. 112-120); there is a glossary (pp. 121-128).

THE EROTIC ELEGIES OF ALBIUS TIBULLUS, transl. Hubert Creekmore. New York: Washington Square Press 1966. Pp. xx, 161; $7.95 cloth.
Bilingual edition; free verse. The introduction (pp. ix-xx) presents a potted survey of ancient elegy and a mechanical catalogue of elegiac conventions (which veers off into a tabulation of Roman religious practices). The notes (pp. 127-146) give a leisurely commentary on each poem, with information often distilled from K.F. Smith's great edition. There is a glossary (pp. 147-161).

Tibullus ought not to daunt translators as Horace or Propertius do; his subtleties lie in the movement of thought within an individual poem, a matter for the critic rather than the translator to unravel. The late Hubert Creekmore's versions succeed precisely because he is as literal as he can be without awkwardness, and his loose metrical form allows him scope to translate without padding or abridgement. There are infelicities (1.1.48 *somnos imbre iuvante sequi* 'wake and doze to raindrop lullabies'; 1.9.18 *saepe solent auro multa subesse mala* 'under gold it's usual often to find many evils') and doubtful renderings (1.1.3 *quem labor adsiduus vicino terreat hoste* 'and daunt approaching foes with the endless toil of war'; 2.4.30 *a Rubro...mari* 'from sun-red seas'), but most of these are venial.

The defects of Carrier's translations are more pervasive, since they spring from her choice of metrical structure. Neither the six-stress nor the three-stress line she uses is a comfortable equivalent for the elegiac couplet: the first necessitates padding, and this introduces unmistakably modern images; the second requires ruthless compression and often produces an unauthentic baldness, or an even more bogus obscurity. One specimen of each metre will illustrate these faults. First, the translation of 1.1.25-32; italics represent expansions or additions:

Here *in this narrow range* (parvo) I shall *savor it wholly* (possim contentus vivere)
never set forth to make journeys *into the darkness*
be sheltered from August's heat in the cool of *apple-tree* shadow
hearing the sound of the brook slipping *like silk* beside me
never *too proud or* ashamed *to hoe an acre and plant it* (tenuisse bidentem),
hurry the slow ox with *a branch for* a goad, or carry
home *in my arms* ewe-lamb or kid *found bleating and frightened*
left by its dam, abandoned, *lost in the underbrush.*

Second the translation of 1.9.29f., followed by the Latin; underscored words have not been rendered:

'I would have denied at your bidding
that rivers run downhill.
When you wept, I believed your weeping,
and credulous, dried your tears.
It's Pholoe now you cherish!'

illis eriperes verbis mihi *sidera caeli*
lucere et pronas fluminis esse vias.

quin etiam flebas: at *non* ego *fallere doctus*
tergebam umentes credulus usque genas.
quid faciam, nisi et ipse fores in amore *puellae?*

Creekmore's translations are thus to be preferred, but the apparatus of his edition is sadly amateurish. It would be agreeable to see his versions re-issued in a more sober (and less expensive) setting, with a new introduction and notes by a competent scholar.

[Other opinion. *Carrier:* M.C.J. Putnam (*CW* 62 [1968] 103), 'smooth, graceful, choice...there will be few excuses for scholars to grumble'. *Creekmore:* M.C.J. Putnam (*CW* 60 [1967] 258), 'serviceable...faithful and exact'.]

VIRGIL, ECLOGUES

⁂ THE ECLOGUES, GEORGICS, AND AENEID OF VIRGIL, transl. C. Day Lewis. London: Oxford University Press 1967. Pp. vii, 529. £0.75; $2.95 paper.

Free verse. This is the only verse translation of the Eclogues now available. It is generally accurate and as literal as possible; the language is plain and modern, with only occasional lapses into 'poetic' diction (e.g., 6.58 *errabunda bovis vestigia* 'the tracks of his stravagueing hoof'; 10.55 *interea mixtis lustrabo Maenala nymphis* 'I'll roam the slopes of Maenalus with bevies of nymphs the while'); and the odd lame phrase (4.1 *paulo maiora canamus* 'I would try now a somewhat grander theme'; 10.44 *insanus amor duri Martis* 'insensate zeal for the War-god'). A better translation in this idiom could hardly be desired. The absence of introduction and notes, though, is a drawback.

[Other opinion. E.C. Woodcock (*Durham University Journal* 25 [1963/64] 53f.) had severe criticism for Lewis's pedestrian language and unstructured metre, but admitted that he captured the sense 'tolerably well'.]

Several nineteenth-century verse renderings of the *Eclogues* remain available: C.S. Calverley (New York: Heritage Books 1961, $6.95), James Rhoades (Oxford: Oxford University Press [World's Classics] 1962, $2.25), and T.F. Royds, M.A. (Dutton Everyman Series 1965, $3.25). All, however, deploy an archaic poetic diction that makes them unsuited for present use. Those who prefer to read Virgil in period costume may use the translation of a true poet, since Dryden's complete Virgil is still in print (Oxford: Oxford University Press [World's Classics] 1961, $2.90).

It should be clear from the foregoing report that few areas of lyric poetry have received definitive treatment but that, with the exception of Hellenistic poetry, none is without serviceable translations. One might hope that the appearance in recent years of reliable texts of early Greek lyric (*Lyrica Graeca Selecta,* ed. D.L. Page, Oxford 1968) and of useful annotated anthologies for students (D.A. Campbell, *Greek Lyric Poetry*, London 1967; D.E. Gerber, *Euterpe*, Amsterdam [Hakkert] 1970) will lead to a modern and comprehensive anthology in translation for this period. In Latin too the time is suitable, because of the several valuable versions of individual poets which have appeared in the last ten years, to put together a collection devoted to the major lyric poets. But the most pressing need in this field, and the one which no volume now available begins to fulfil, is for editions of lyric poets that combine careful translation with detailed and informed literary criticism.

R.J. Tarrant
University College, Toronto
September, 1971

ADDENDUM. Since the time of writing, James Michie's translation of Catullus has been issued in a paper-back edition (London: Panther Books 1972. £0.40; $1.25 in Canada), thus fulfilling the wish expressed in my review.

NOTES

1. As was done, for example, by A.D. Godley, *CR* 37 (1923) 167f.

2. My sources have been the *Index Translationum*, the 1970 volumes of *Books in Print*, the useful bibliographical survey by U. Schoenheim in *ACR* 1 (1971) 9-41, and communications from publishers.

3. The references to *PMG* and *PLF*, however, are garbled: on p. 301 'Page' is missing at the head of the appropriate column, and on p. 301-304 'Lobel and Page' is a mistake: read 'Page'.

4. The failure to render *κατεδύσαμεν* is one of several signs that Sinclair at times worked from Paton's English rather than from the Greek.

5. This may be seen from the introduction: Archilochus is 'the second poet of the West'; Archilochus was a mercenary; iambic verse is his invention; 'to the ancients...he was The Satirist'; 'we have not a single whole poem of Archilochus'; 'Horace, imitating Archilochus, congratulated himself on bringing Greek numbers into Italy'; reference is made to a 'Pausanius'.

6. 'Since such difficulties [as the place of *Ol.* 6.84f.] are common in the Pindaric text, we obviously cannot deal with them in the preparatory essays as difficulties, but must gloss them over; the solution must appear as though there had been no problem at all but merely a self-evident step or item in the counterpoised parts of the poem.' (p. 14).

7. Lattimore omits L.-P. 94.

8. The extensive section devoted to Sappho in Barnstone's *Greek Lyric Poetry* contains the nucleus of the separate edition entitled *Sappho. Lyrics in the Original Greek with Translations* (New York: New York University Press 1965. Pp. xxxii, 208; $6.00). This edition possesses an extensive apparatus of varying usefulness and reliability; the Greek texts printed show the influence of Edmonds more than Page or Lobel, and restorations are not always marked (e.g., Edmonds 82).

9. I omit Davenport's supplement for the missing first line: 'Before my lying heart could speak for life'. A note records the literal meaning

of *τεθνάκην 'αδόλως θέλω* as if an irrelevant piece of antiquarian lore.

10. An exception is 11.43, where Mills retains Gow's 'leave the sea to beat' for *ἔα*.

11. His dependence reveals itself amusingly at 1.130 where *ὑπ''Ερωτος ἐς 'Αιδαν ἕλκομαι*, rendered by Gow 'to Hades am I haled by Love', appears in Mills as 'Love calls me now to Hades'.

12. On the Lesbia-poems: 'we shall probably never know just how "true" the poems are, in terms of a real-life love affair. And it is of little consequence whether they are "true" or not, in that sense. What *is* important is the success with which they exploit the poetic possibilities of such a relationship' (p. 18).

13. 1, 3, 5, 13, 26, 31, 38, 46, 72, 84, 96, 101, 116.

14. M.G. Balme and M.S. Warren, *Aestimanda* (Oxford: Oxford University Press 1965), pp. 41f., 49f.

15. The boundaries of the two types are not rigid; I would place in the cummingsesque group 1, 2, 3, 5, 7, 13, 16, 31, 46, 49, 93, 96, 101, and in the other 4, 6, 10, 17, 22, 53.

16. And, be it added, the smirky circumlocutions Copley substitutes for Catullus's exact sexual vocabulary: e.g., 16.11 *qui duros nequeunt movere lumbos* 'who've kinda lost/the swing of things'; 58.5 *glubit* 'she hauls ashes'; 59.1 *fellat* 'what she and little cousin Rufus/is doing together ain't pretty'. On the other hand, Copley's 'Dickie-boy' for *Mentula* deserves commendation.

17. The echo of *Richard II* is not the only obtrusive allusion in these versions, or the worst; the palm must go to 34.1f., 'Boys and girls, we pledge allegiance/to the moon'.

18. Gregory is not seldom more blunt or leeringly elliptical than Ovid, e.g., 1.3.22; 1.5.8, 21, 24; 1.9.1, 7, 19, 27, 39f., 46, etc.

19. The notes, however, will be more helpful to classical students than to those who consult this edition for its translation. Of Lee's own conjectures only *formosam* for *fortunam* in 2.19.7 exerts strong attraction (the others are *aut* for *ut* in 1.7.55, *tantum* for *vatum* in 3.9.29).

20. Lapses in this department generally mirror uncertainty about Propertius's meaning, e.g., 4.4.20, 4.11.8.

21. See on these points the recent discussion by R.O.A.M. Lyne, *PCPS* N.S. 16 (1970) 64.

22. Comparable is the distortion of a Propertian phrase into a cliché: 1.1.1 *Cynthia prima suis...me cepit ocellis* 'no girl but Cynthia ever caught my eye'; 1.3.7 *talis visa mihi mollem spirare quietem* 'so did my Cynthia seem the soul of rest'.

23. In fairness let it be noted that this error was committed by Butler in his Loeb translation.

24. While this marks an immense improvement over, for example, Carrier's use of Butler's Loeb edition, it is unfortunate that Warden did not emancipate himself from the dubious or erroneous interpretations sometimes offered by Camps (e.g. at 1.3.24ff., 1.16.23, 1.21.6, 4.11.72, 102).

25. I have as yet noticed no egregious errors, and the number of minor inaccuracies appears tolerable (e.g., 1.3.8 *non certis* 'unresisting'; 3.1.23 *omnia...fingit maiora* 'make all things grow'; 3.13.37 *lentas (umbras)* 'gentle'; 3.13.65-66, 4.4.20, 4.7.6, 4.11.5-6, 16, 30, 74, 99).

26. Elsewhere allusions are omitted, e.g. 1.1.11 *Partheniis*; 14 *Arcadiis*; 1.3.1 *Thesea*; 6 *Apidano*; 42 *Orpheae.*

INDEX

INDEX OF PUBLISHERS

Argonaut, *Ancient Greek Literature in Translation* 10

Bobbs-Merrill: Catullus 27ff., (Horace) 38ff., Martial 41ff., Propertius 52f., Sappho 20ff.

California, University of: Archilochus 15f., Sappho 20ff.
Cape Groliard, Catullus 36f.
Chicago, University of: *Greek Lyrics* 7f., Horace 38ff., Pindar 17ff.

Dutton, Catullus 35f.
Dutton (Everyman): *Greek Poetry* 8f., Virgil, *Eclogues* 58

Grove, Catullus 33ff.

Harcourt, Brace, Martial 44f.
Harper and Row, *Greek Literature in Translation* 10
Hart-Davies, Rupert, Catullus 27
Heritage, Virgil, *Eclogues* 58
Houghton Mifflin, *Latin Poetry in Verse Translation* 25f.

Indiana, University of: *Greek Lyric Poetry* 5ff., Martial 41ff., Ovid, *Amores* 47, Propertius 50ff., Tibullus 55ff.

Littlefield, Adams, *Classics of Roman Literature* 26
Longmans, *Greek and Roman Literature in Translation* 10

MacGibbon and Kee, Catullus 33
Macmillan, Greek Anthology 11ff.
(McClelland and Stewart, Greek Anthology 11ff.)
McKay, *Roman Literature in Translation* 26
Methuen, Greek Anthology 11ff.
Michigan, University of: Catullus 30ff., Greek Anthology 11ff., Pindar 17ff., Sappho 20ff.
Murray, John, Ovid, *Amores* 47ff.

New American Library: Martial 43f., Ovid, *Amores* 46ff., Sappho 21ff.
New Directions, Greek Anthology 11ff.
New York University, Sappho 60 (n.8)

Oklahoma, University of: Horace 40
Oxford: (*Latin Poetry in Verse Translation* 25f.), *Oxford Book of Greek Verse in Translation* 9f., Virgil, *Eclogues* (3) 58

(Panther, Catullus 59)

Penguin: Catullus 32f., Pindar 17ff., Propertius 50ff., *Roman Readings* 26
Prentice-Hall, *Classics of Greek Literature* 10
Purdue: Catullus 29f., Martial 41ff., Theocritus 24

(Schocken, *Greek Lyric Poetry* 5ff.)

Toronto, University of: *Swans and Amber* 10

Viking: (Ovid, *Amores* 47ff.), *Portable Greek Reader* 10, *Portable Greek Reader* 26

(Washington, University of, Greek Anthology 11ff.)
Washington Square: Horace 38ff., Tibullus 55ff.
Wesleyan University, Martial 44f.

INDEX OF TRANSLATORS

Auden, W.H. (ed.), *Portable Greek Reader* 10

Barnard, Mary, Sappho 20ff.
Barnstone, Willis: *Greek Lyric Poetry* 5ff., Sappho 60 (n.8),
Bovie, Palmer, Martial 43f.
Bowra, C.M. (ed.): *Oxford Book of Greek Verse in Translation* 9f., Pindar 17ff.

Calverley, C.S., Virgil, *Eclogues* 58
Carrier, Constance: Propertius 50ff., Tibullus 55ff.
Clancy, Joseph P., Horace 38ff.
Copley, Frank O., Catullus 30ff.
Creekmore, Hubert, Tibullus 55ff.

Davenport, B. (ed.), *Portable Roman Reader* 26
Davenport, Guy: Archilochus 15f., Sappho 20ff.
Dryden, John, Virgil, *Eclogues* 58

Fitts, Dudley: Greek Anthology 11ff., Martial 44f.

Grant, Michael (ed.), *Roman Readings* 26
Gregory, Horace: Catullus 33ff., Ovid, *Amores* 46ff.
Groden, Suzy Q., Sappho 20ff.
Guinagh, K. (ed.), *Roman Literature in Translation* 26

Henze, Helen R., Horace 40
Higham, T.F. (ed.), *Oxford Book of Greek Verse in Translation* 9f.
Howe, George (ed.), *Greek Literature in Translation* 10
Humphries, Rolph: Martial 41ff., Ovid, *Amores* 47

Lattimore, Richmond: Greek *Lyrics* 7f., Pindar 17ff.
Lee, Guy, Ovid, *Amores* 47ff.
Lewis, C. Day, Virgil, *Eclogues* 58
Lind, L.R. (ed.), *Latin Poetry in Verse Translation* 25f.

Lucas, F.L., *Greek Poetry* 8f.

Marcellino, Ralph, Martial 41ff.
Matheson, William H., Pindar 17ff.
Michie, James: Catullus 27, 59, Horace 38ff.
Mills, Bariss: Catullus 29f., Martial 41ff., Theocritus 24
Murray, Philip, Martial 44f.
Myers, Reney, Catullus 35f.

Oates, Whitney J. (ed.), *Greek and Roman Literature in Translation*
Ormsby, Robert J., Catullus 35f.

Rexroth, Kenneth, *Greek Anthology* 11ff.
Rhoades, James Virgil, *Eclogues* 58
Richards, Lewis A., *Ancient Greek Literature in Translation* 10
Roche, Paul, Sappho 21ff.
Royds, T.F., Virgil, *Eclogues* 58
Ruck, Carl A.P., Pindar 17ff.

Sinclair, Andrew, Greek Anthology 11ff.
Sisson, C.H., Catullus 33
Skelton, Robin, Greek Anthology 12ff.
Swanson, Roy Arthur, Catullus 27ff.

Thompson, Dorothy B., *Swans and Amber* 10

Warden, John, Propertius 52f.
Watts, A.E., Propertius 50ff.
Wedeck, H.E. (ed.): *Classics of Greek Literature* 10,
Classics of Roman Literature 26
Whigham, Peter, Catullus 32f.

Zukofsky, Celia and Louis, Catullus 36f.